sew + quilt

techniques + projects for hand-stitching + patchwork

A BEGINNER'S GUIDE

SUSAN BEAL

The Taunton Press

Text © 2019 by Susan Beal

Photographs © 2019 by Steve Wanke

Illustrations © 2019 by The Taunton Press, Inc.

The Taunton Press
Inspiration for hands-on living®

The Taunton Press, Inc., 63 South Main Street, PO Box 5506, Newtown, CT 06470-5506

Email: tp@taunton.com

Editor: Carolyn Mandarano

Copy Editor: Betty Christiansen

Indexer: Barbara Mortenson

Jacket/Cover design: Kimberly Adis

Interior design: Kimberly Adis

Layout: Kimberly Adis

Photographer: Steve Wanke

Stylist: Shannon Quimby

Illustrators: Michelle Freedman, Alexis Hartman

Props: courtesy of The Bull & the Bee (bullandbeebaby.com) and Collage
(collagepdx.com)

The following names/manufacturers appearing in *sew + quilt* are trademarks:
Black & Decker™, Kona®, Lumograph®, Mettler®, Olfa® Endurance™, Pendleton®,
Pink Pearl®, Post-it® Notes, QuilTak™, Quilters Dream Green™, Ruby Ruler™,
Schmetz®, Sharpie®, SideWinder™, Sisters Outdoor Quilt Show™, Staedtler Mars®

Library of Congress Cataloging-in-Publication Data

Names: Beal, Susan, author.

Title: Sew + quilt : techniques + projects for hand-stitching + patchwork,
   a beginner's guide / Susan Beal.

Other titles: Sew and quilt

Description: Newtown, CT : The Taunton Press, Inc., [2019] | Includes index.

Identifiers: LCCN 2018025502 | ISBN 9781631869365

Subjects: LCSH: Patchwork quilts. | Patchwork--Patterns. | Quilting--Patterns.

Classification: LCC TT835 .B29255 2019 | DDC 746.46/041--dc23

LC record available at https://lccn.loc.gov/2018025502

Printed in the United States of America

10 9 8 7 6 5 4 3 2 1

dedication

FOR MY TWO BRIGHTEST
STARS, PEARL & EVERETT

acknowledgments

SEW + QUILT HAS BEEN MY MOST PERSONAL BOOK by far, and I wrote and sewed everything for it over a very eventful year. The kindness, support, creativity, and encouragement so many people shared with me along the way were a huge gift.

When my editor, Carolyn Mandarano, asked if I'd like to write a sewing and quilting book for her, I had a million ideas. We worked together to thoughtfully narrow all of them down to what you see here, and her insights, feedback, and vision all shaped those evolving ideas into a book I'm so proud of. My agent, Stacey Glick, is always such a wonderful advocate, and I appreciate her guidance and support.

My art director, Rosalind Loeb, offered such precision in bringing everything visual to life, from the photography to the page design. Special thanks to our photographer, Steve Wanke; his assistant, Adam Michaels; our amazing stylist, Shannon Quimby; and her collaborators, Tasha Bartley and Puji Sherer, for their gorgeous contributions, working in the sunny, inviting mid-century palette I love best.

Alexis Hartman has illustrated my last seven books, and I treasure our long partnership. My Little Star Mini-Quilt is for her new baby, Camille. My longtime Portland Modern Quilt Guild (PMQG) friend Michelle Freedman stepped in to illustrate the embroidery, sewing, and quilting techniques with her fresh perspective, making each step beautiful as well as crystal clear.

Thank you to Ariga, Nichole, and everyone at Robert Kaufman Fabrics, and my deep thanks to Melody Miller, Kim Kight, Monica Solorio-Snow, and Elizabeth Hartman for their wonderful prints and friendship, and to Kelly Cole for the very fun swap of vintage sheet squares. Thanks so much to Amanda and Alex at Quilt Canvas for creating such an amazing quilt design program, and to Liana, Courtney, and everyone at Creativebug for the chance to teach some of my favorite projects there!

My longarm quilter Nancy Stovall finished so many of my big quilts so beautifully, and her husband, Matthew, also specially photographed my S+Q embroidery sampler on p. 18 with such thoughtfulness and detail.

My friends Rebecca Ringquist, Jenn Sturiale, Kelly Cole, Denyse Schmidt, Nancy, and Michelle shared such great advice for the beginning stitcher, making this the book I wish I'd had when I was learning how to sew. And my Instagram friends and blog readers have been so encouraging and offered enthusiastic feedback on the colorful bits and pieces I've shared along the way.

Thanks to my many PMQG friends who cheered me on: Heather, Petra, Amber, Tamara, Kelly, Rebecca, Nancy, Michelle, Kim, MaryAnn, Robin, Jessica, Erin, Kimberly, Judy, Barbara, Angie, and so many others. And for my friends who don't sew, but think the things I make are so cool—thanks for always being excited with me!

Finally, my family inspires me every day. Thank you to my mom, Jeanie, who loves my quilts, and my husband, Andrew, who always encourages my creativity and loves me unconditionally. And to my two bright stars who constantly inspire me: my colorful, creative daughter, Pearl, and my sunny, joyful little boy, Everett.

Last, thank you to everyone who has picked up one of my books and tried something new. I hope *sew + quilt* brings you joy and many happy hours of sewing.

contents

introduction

SEWING, ALONG WITH QUILTING AND EMBROIDERY, changed my life, but I didn't learn how to sew until I was 26. I had taken art classes all my life, and I have always loved making things, but my sewing skills were limited to a basic running stitch and a few long-ago childhood cross-stitch projects. I had no idea how to thread a machine, follow a sewing pattern, or piece a quilt block. I always wished I'd learned how to sew as a kid, but it seemed so complicated and overwhelming that I didn't even know where to start.

Then my best friend, Fiona, came to visit me in Portland for a week, and she taught me how to sew on a vintage aqua Singer I found for $20, with all the enthusiasm, patience, and kindness a beginner needs. I tried new things, messed up, ripped out the seams, pressed my fabric, and tried again. And once I got my confidence up, it was so exciting. I vividly remember that amazing feeling of suddenly being able to make anything I wanted—night and day from just a week earlier.

A few years later, I nervously tried my hand at patchwork for the first time, and once I got used to the new teeny-tiny ¼-in. seam allowance, I made two improvisationally pieced log cabin pillows for my couch and dreamed up a million more ideas. I made my very first quilt for my mom's birthday over the next few weeks, started an anniversary quilt for my husband and me after that, and really never stopped.

So whether you're a complete beginner, just like I was, you already know how to sew but want to try some new patchwork quilting or embroidery projects, or you're an all-around sewing superstar who's looking for a fun and easy quilt to whip up in a weekend, *sew + quilt* is for you! I wanted to write the book I really wish I'd had when I was learning, so I asked some of my favorite quilters, sewists, and embroidery artists to share *their* best advice for beginners, too.

First, you'll learn five simple embroidery stitches and four beginner-friendly quilt blocks by making two hands-on Sew + Quilt Samplers. In the first section, your practice of marking lines and stitching on plain fabric becomes a pretty embroidery to display in a hoop, and in the next, your first four patchwork blocks come together in a pretty little mini-quilt. Then, after finishing these two modern samplers and building your skills and confidence, you're ready to take on any project in the book and make it your own, from colorful embroidery to beautiful bed quilts!

With the pressures of work, family, and personal life, I know it can be difficult to find time for a creative hobby. But even a few minutes of handwork like embroidery, sewing, or quilting nurtures mindfulness, much like meditation does. Creativity can feel very elusive in a busy, modern life crowded with work, digital distractions, and chores, especially in our increasingly dark and polarized world. But when we sew or embroider—even the simplest project—the process reconnects us with our creative hearts while calming some of the rushing anxiety that seems to be the backdrop of modern life.

Making something special for a dear friend or to use every day in your own home is a double gift—the practice of stitching that calms and centers, followed by the true happiness of enjoying something beautiful, made with your own hands. I hope you'll be inspired to create your own versions of my quilts and samplers using your favorite colors and prints.

I've been so lucky to meet some wonderful modern quilters, sewists, and embroidery artists online (via message boards, swaps, Flickr groups, and Instagram hashtags) and through my local guild, Portland Modern Quilt Guild, and they provided creative inspiration, ideas, and friendship.

I've set up a site, sewplusquilt.com, where I share a bit of that creative community and where I've added everything I couldn't squeeze into this book, things like alternative versions of my favorite projects and lots of ideas for framing your embroidery, making special labels for your quilts, and displaying your handmade work. You'll also find printable coloring sheets for lots of my book quilts (so you can play with different layouts and color combinations) and get the chance to try designing your own quilts on Quilt Canvas and take quilting classes on Creativebug. Please visit me there, or post your projects on Instagram tagged #sewplusquilt to say hello. I'd love to see what you're making, and I hope that you'll share your creativity with everyone else, too!

tools + materials

SO MUCH OF THE JOY OF SEWING IS WORKING WITH GOOD
tools and beautiful materials, but it can be a bit
intimidating to pick out all the solids and prints for a
quilt or the colors for
your first embroidery
project. I hope
this introduction
to fabric, supplies,
embellishments, and
more can shine a little
light on not only *how*
to get started, but also
what might work best
in your version of any
(or all!) of my designs.

quilting cotton

FABRIC ESSENTIALS

QUILTING COTTON

Quilting cotton is wonderful for sewing and piecing patchwork, as well as for hand-stitching and hand-quilting. Most quilting cottons fall somewhere in the range of medium-weight fine-weave cotton, but as you shop, touch, or "swatch" fabrics, you'll notice that the fabric's *hand* can be very different from one brand or designer to another. The hand is literally how the fabric feels to the touch, but it also translates into how it drapes, presses, and sews. Some quilting cottons are a light, almost fluid weight with a silky feel, while others are a sturdier broadcloth with a more textured finish. They're all designed to work well in patchwork projects, so try different brands of solids or print collections to see which ones you enjoy working with most.

Many designers create one or two collections a year, with a mix of signature prints and supporting players. Fabric companies now often pair their designers' collections with matching or coordinating solids, which takes some of the guesswork out of pairing fabrics for the rest of us.

When you're planning a sewing or quilting project, using prints from the same collection or designer will give a smooth, cohesive overall feel in terms of color and pattern. However, there's a lot of charm to scrappiness—using a variety of different prints (and solids, too) for a fresh, unexpected appeal.

Most quilting cottons off the bolt measure about 42 in. to 44 in. wide, including selvages on each side. For the purposes of this book, however, I've written project yardage requirements as 40 in. wide, so that any shrinkage or loss of selvage is easily accounted for and won't cut into your fabric. I usually don't wash contemporary quilting cottons before sewing or quilting with them, but if you're making clothes, always prewash your fabrics to make sure they shrink *before* you sew a fitted garment! Quilting cottons are perfect for layering, making homemade custom binding for a full-size or mini-quilt, piecing, backing, and embroidery.

DENIM

Denim varies greatly, from soft lightweight or medium-weight chambray to heavy, durable, and densely woven options, and from typical light-to-dark blues to overdyes, brights, metallics, stretch denim, and more. For the beginning sewist and quilter, I recommend lighter-weight 100% cotton denim since it's easier to work with and pieces and topstitches very nicely. It's also ideal for hand embroidery and offers a gorgeous setting for any palette of colorful floss. In my denim projects (like my Sashiko Drawstring Bag on p. 68 and Basketweave Picnic Quilt on p. 94), I used 6½-oz., 8-oz., or 10-oz. indigo denims from Robert Kaufman, which are sturdy but piece and press more like a quilting cotton than a heavy outerwear or home décor denim. Many denims measure wider than typical quilting cottons do, 58 in. to 60 in. across as yardage. If you're using denim as binding, test it with a sample strip before cutting for an entire project; it may not double fold and press as smoothly as a lighter cotton.

denim

LINENS AND BLENDS

One hundred percent linen and linen blends are a rich, textured option for special sewing and patchwork. They wash well, hand- or machine-stitch beautifully, and have an inviting texture that creases and flows nicely (perfectionists may feel differently!). I always use a light spray starch when piecing and pressing linen fabrics, which keeps them smooth and neat. Vintage linens can be beautiful, but modern ones like the Essex Linens I used in my Flying in Pairs Quilt (p. 99) are a joy to sew with. Linen comes in a range of neutral colors as well as a rainbow of colors and even a subtle sparkle weave with metallic threads.

VINTAGE FABRICS AND SHEETS

Create a truly unique project or quilt by using vintage fabrics or vintage sheets. They sew well in combination with quilting cottons (in my Bright Star Quilt on p. 126, I mixed three dozen vintage sheets and fabrics with new prints as half-square triangles) and are a lot of fun to play with. Vintage sheets are often wonderfully soft from washing and are ready to use. But if you find deadstock (never used) yardage or scraps of vintage fabrics, I recommend prewashing them before you piece or sew with them, since some older dyes aren't as stable as the ones in contemporary fabrics. My friend Kelly Cole's online shop, Vintage Fabric Studio, has amazing options ready to sew with.

MUSLIN

Lightweight and inexpensive, muslin is a cotton fabric available in white, off-white, and unbleached neutral colors. It's perfect for backing an embroidery project, foundation piecing like string quilting blocks, or testing a project before cutting into your special fabrics. I recommend having a few yards on hand for basics, and with its plain, neutral hues, it's fun to stitch on, too!

linens + vintage fabric

RECYCLED GARMENTS

Blue jeans, woven cotton shirts, wool coats, and other pieces of apparel can be very affordable (and environmentally friendly) options for sewing and quilting. Reusing old jeans or corduroy pants by cutting the still-sturdy sections into strips and squares is a great upcycle, for example, whether they are your own or purchased from a thrift store or yard sale. You can find colorful secondhand or vintage garments at thrift stores or estate sales, and salvage generous swaths of fabric from the back, front, and sleeves of a man's button-down shirt or from a long skirt. And special clothes handed down from a grandmother or parent or saved from your kids' outgrown favorites can create a very meaningful gift like a mini-quilt or pillow, or mix into a larger quilt.

▣ **Another Idea** *from* Kelly Cole

Sewing with vintage sheets is a lot of fun, especially with a few tips and tricks to get you started. Vintage sheets are often made from a 50/50 cotton-polyester blend, so they need a little extra care when ironing. Use an iron set to "blend" or "wool"—lower than the hotter cotton setting—so you don't damage the fabric and leave your iron with a sticky residue. Spray starch gives your sheet fabric crisp stability before cutting and keeps your seams neat within patchwork.

WOOL

I love wool, but I was a little nervous the first time I worked with it, even after years of confidently sewing with other fabrics. Once I learned a few tricks for keeping things going smoothly, I realized that it cuts, presses, pieces, and topstitches like butter, with a rich, gorgeous finish like no other material. Whether you're using wool scraps, reclaimed garments, or yardage for your sewing and patchwork, the finished project will become a modern heirloom to share with friends or family. For unmatched quality, I always recommend Pendleton wool fabrics, which are all woven in Oregon and Washington. The Pendleton Woolen Mill Store has a mail-order business (see Resources on p. 153).

wool

PRECUTS OR YARDAGE?

PRECUTS

Precuts are an easy way to get started on a project with a fabric collection or color family of solids you're excited about. Instead of buying many individual fabrics one by one, you can start with a quilting-friendly set of strips, squares, or cuts in various measurements, so a variety of prints or solids are ready to work with.

Jelly rolls/roll-ups are a neatly rolled set of assorted fabrics cut into strips 2½ in. x width of fabric (WOF, which is usually 44 in. with selvages), perfect for rail fence, log cabin, or string piecing. One of my favorite projects is my Floating Crosses Quilt (p. 90). I pieced the string blocks that form the crosses from a single roll-up of my friend Elizabeth Hartman's Terrarium fabric collection.

Charm squares are a neat stack of 5-in. squares, great for half-square triangles (HSTs) or oversized log cabin centers. They make a fun and striking pillow cover like the one on p. 72.

Fat quarters (FQs) are a nice size for patchwork, approximately 18 in. x 22 in. (including a selvage on one edge). A standard ¼-yd. cut of fabric would measure 9 in. x WOF, for a very long, narrow piece to work with. A fat quarter offers a more generous, boxy

rectangle of a single fabric for sewing or quilting. Many quilting shops sell FQs individually, and manufacturers often package a stack of folded FQs from a single collection or themed mix of solids.

Fat eighths are 9 in. x 22 in. rather than the 4½ in. x WOF that a standard ⅛ yd. measures.

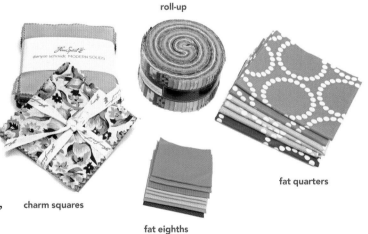

roll-up

fat quarters

charm squares

fat eighths

FABRIC YARDAGE

Yardage just means a larger cut of fabric off the bolt, often measured in increments of a yard (36 in./3 ft.). Half yards are useful in creating patchwork quilt blocks or to bind a larger bed quilt. Larger quantities, like a yard or more of continuous uncut fabric, are ideal for backgrounds, sashing or borders, or piecing as backs. I like to organize my fabrics that measure ½ yd. or larger off the bolt by folding them a second time so the center fold meets the selvages, then wrapping the double-folded fabric around an acid-free piece of cardboard—a technique I learned from quilter Angela Pingel. You can secure the fabric with a straight pin or a piece of washi tape. Then, arrange them vertically side by side like books on a shelf (see p. 13) or stack them horizontally (see p. 5), so you can see the print for color matching or inspiration.

OTHER ESSENTIALS FOR PATCHWORK + QUILTING

BATTING

There are many brands, types, and weights of batting, but for bed quilts, pillows, or smaller projects, I like to use 100% cotton batting with a small amount of loft. For wall quilts or others that will be displayed vertically, I recommend a relatively flat, lightweight batting with scrim—a subtle woven grid that adds sturdiness so that the finished quilt holds its shape and definition nicely. And for special, cozy quilts, a wool batting is amazing. Save your batting scraps to make mini-quilts, pillow covers, and potholders.

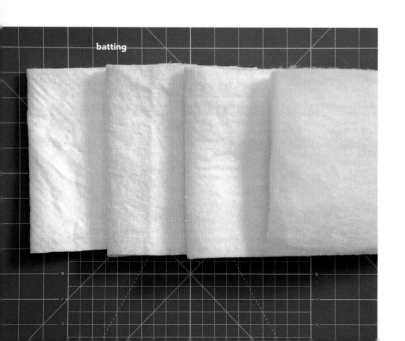
batting

QUILT BACKS

You can use any quilting cotton or similar weight fabric to make a back for a mini-quilt or pillow. For larger quilts that measure wider than the typical 40 in. of a quilting cotton, you can piece your own back by joining fabrics together to achieve a large enough size. I recommend using a ½-in. seam allowance to join larger sections, to support the full weight of the fabrics. You can also use good-condition vintage or new sheets, or extra-wide quilt back fabrics, which are sold in widths of 90 in. to 108 in. off the bolt. Simply buy the number of yards you need for the length of your quilt top.

ESSENTIAL TOOLS

To get started with any of the projects in this book, you'll need some basic supplies. These fall into a couple of different categories: embroidery tools, sewing and quilting tools, and tools that are nice to have but aren't required. I create "kits" of these tools so that I have everything at my fingertips before I start a project.

EMBROIDERY KIT

• **Quilting cotton, linen, or muslin.** Two layers of fabric are ideal, cut 2 in. to 3 in. bigger than the embroidery hoop or finished project. The back layer of fabric can be inexpensive neutral-colored muslin; it isn't meant to be seen, so don't use beautiful or expensive fabric here!

• **Embroidery hoops** in the size of your choice. I like using anything from a small 3-in.-dia. hoop up through about 8 in. Inexpensive wooden hoops are easy to use, and then you can paint or embellish them to "frame" and display your finished work, if you like. The Sew + Quilt Embroidery Sampler on p. 18 uses a 7-in. hoop, so make sure to include one of those.

• **Needles.** Be sure to use good-quality needles designed for embroidery rather than hand-sewing with standard thread. I like embroidery, crewel, and sashiko needles. A needle threader is also handy for threading a thicker strand or multiple strands through the eye of a needle.

embroidery kit

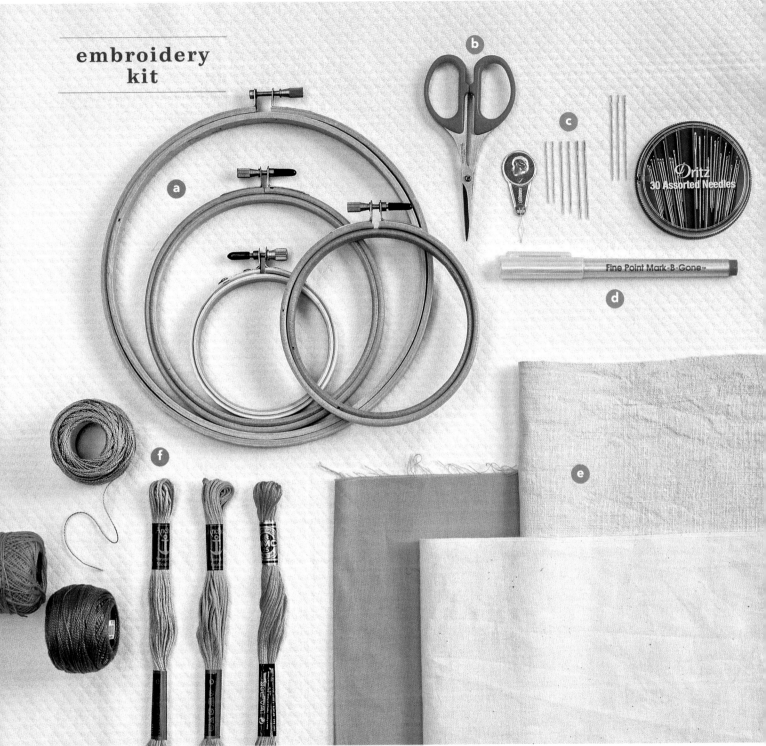

a embroidery hoops • **b** scissors • **c** needles
d fabric marker • **e** quilting cotton, linen, and muslin • **f** perle cotton and floss

9

Another Idea *from* Jenn Sturiale of Stitcharama

Embroidery floss comes in so many colors and textures, but once you're swimming in skeins of stranded floss and balls of perle cotton, you'll find it can get jumbled and knotted all too easily. Easy to use and neat to store, plastic or paper bobbins from the craft store are my favorite way to keep my embroidery threads tidy and accessible. For floss, find the center of a skein, remove both paper tabs, then wind the floss around the bobbin; tuck the end into the notch on the side, and you're done. For perle cotton, just unwind the single strand right off the ball to evenly wrap it around the bobbin. Store your colorful bobbins in portable plastic boxes.

• **Perle cotton or floss.** I love to use perle cotton, which is a single strand of rich, soft cotton, in size 8 or 12. The quality and colors are beautiful, and the line it creates is full and distinctive. It usually comes wound on a cardboard cone, as a ball of all one color. Floss is usually less expensive and includes six thin strands of the same color of embroidery thread, looped together into a labeled skein, which you separate out (often two strands at a time) for stitching. Metallic flosses and other specialty types, like variegated flosses, are also available and make a beautiful accent to a project.

• **Fabric marker.** This water-soluble or disappearing marker makes freehand writing or drawing, or tracing designs for stitching, very easy. Be sure to always test it on a scrap of fabric first and thoroughly rinse the marks away before pressing or framing.

• **Scissors.** Small, sharp scissors are very handy to have. I like to have a pair threaded on a ribbon so I can wear it around my neck.

SEWING + QUILTING KIT

This kit of sewing and quilting tools will serve you well as you work on more and more projects. You don't have to buy expensive tools and materials from day one, but here are some recommendations for what's worth investing in for the long run.

• **Thread.** Good-quality, new cotton or polyester sewing thread is one of your most important supplies. Buy larger spools of white and neutral colors (tan or off-white), as well as black or navy if you're sewing with a lot of darker fabrics. These subtle workhorse colors are perfect for your piecing and inside seams, where they won't show. Then, choose a compatible or exact color match for your thread for topstitching, quilting, binding, or other decorative elements, so your finished piece looks polished and smooth. I like Gütermann and Mettler sewing thread.

• **Machine needles.** I recommend universal (90/14) or Microtex (sharp) needles for standard sewing and piecing, jeans or denim needles (70/10 or 100/16) for heavier fabrics like wools and denims, and quilting needles (75/11) for machine-quilting through multiple layers. Schmetz is my favorite brand, but others are certainly good, too.

• **Straight pins.** I like larger quilting-style straight pins with bright yellow heads because they're easy to see, but smaller glass- or flower-top pins work, too. I keep my pins on a vintage saucer with magnets glued to the underside, which holds the pins in place nicely but allows you to pick them up one by one.

• **Sewing machine.** A beginner-friendly machine that's sturdy and has a good, solid straight stitch will take you far. I bought my current Pfaff new 12 years ago, and it's been a perfect companion for me as I sew both professionally and just for fun. Look into new or refurbished sewing machines with warranties. A tune-up once a year, along with any other maintenance recommended in your owner's manual, will keep most machines happy.

sewing + quilting kit

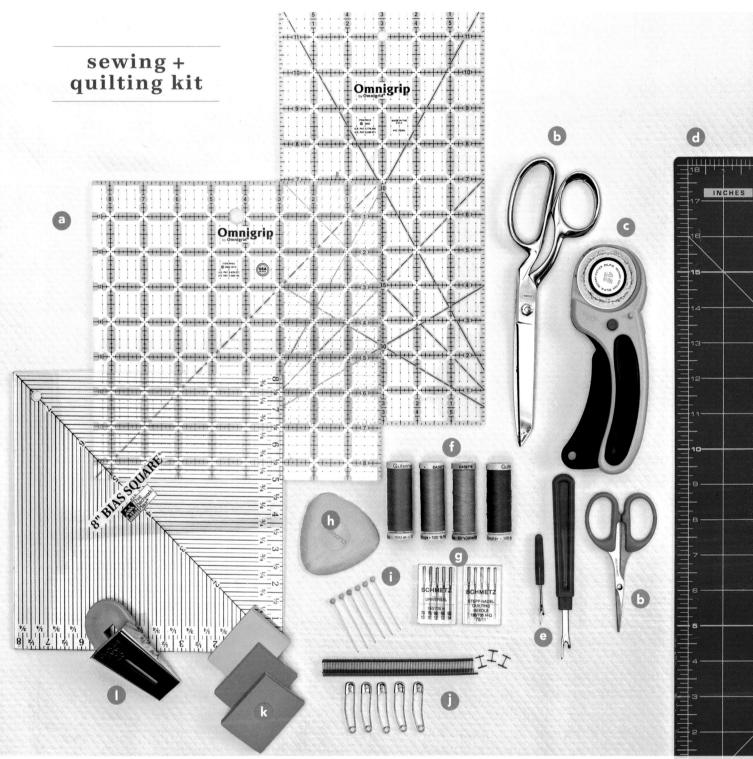

a quilting rulers • **b** scissors • **c** rotary cutter • **d** cutting mat • **e** seam ripper • **f** thread • **g** machine needles
h tailor's chalk • **i** straight pins • **j** safety pins and QuilTak baster tabs • **k** Post-it Notes • **l** bias/binding tape marker

11

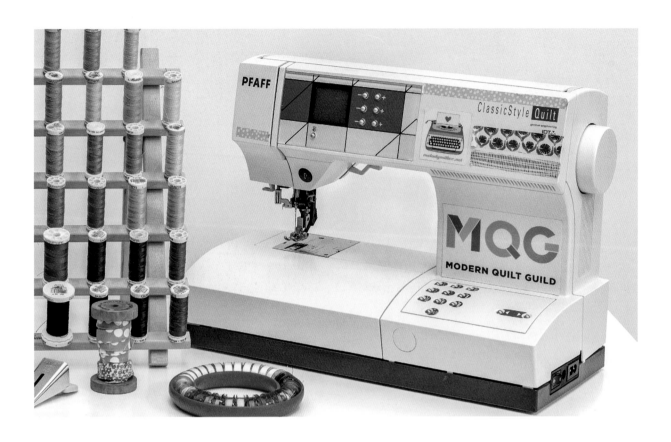

Another Idea *from* Michelle Freedman

Don't forget to change your machine needle to keep your stitches even and straight. I recommend a new needle for every four to six hours of sewing. And be sure to use the right needles for your fabric weight and type. If I'm sewing with denim or wool and then switch to quilting cotton, I put the heavyweight needle back into its case with the flat side of the needle facing out. That way I know it's been used but still has another project's worth of life left in it.

• **Iron with spray bottles of water and/or light spray starch.** Ask friends or look at reviews, and choose a good-quality basic steam iron with all the usual settings, like poly/blend, wool, cotton, and linen. I have an inexpensive Black & Decker iron that presses beautifully. I like to have spray bottles of both distilled water and light spray starch handy, too. Water releases the creases in cotton and aligns the fibers of wool, allowing them to be pressed beautifully, and starch keeps cotton and linen neat. Always test starch on a scrap of a new fabric before using it; it's not ideal for wool or some decorative embellishments.

• **Scissors.** Buy a pair of good-quality full-size scissors that are *only* for cutting fabric.

• **Seam ripper.** This small tool is perfect for easily and quickly removing stitches from an uneven or inaccurate seam, binding join, or quilting line.

• **Rotary cutter.** I like to use a full-size 45-mm rotary cutter for any weight of fabrics. A smaller one is nice for a portable sewing kit. Carefully change rotary blades when they get dull and won't cut through multiple layers of fabric. My favorites are Olfa Endurance blades.

• **Quilting rulers.** I use a 24-in. by 5-in. clear ruler with a lip that fits neatly over the edge of my cutting mat for accurately cutting longer strips of fabric (like selvage to selvage or WOF), a 6-in. by 12-in. flat ruler for smaller projects, and square rulers for squaring up or trimming quilt blocks. Look for clear rulers with easily readable inch and centimeter measurements. I designed many of the quilt blocks in this book with just two sizes of square rulers (8 in. and 8½ in. square). If you're going to invest in any square rulers, I recommend those two. Bias/diagonal line markings (like my 8-in.-square ruler shown on p. 11), make it much easier to line up 45-degree angle piecing like HST and string blocks and to accurately trim them to the finished block size.

• **Cutting mat.** If you have the space, I recommend a 24-in. x 36-in. cutting mat. Mine is right under my machine, so I can cut on the left part of my table and sew just a few inches away. If your sewing setup is smaller, an 18-in. x 24-in. mat is a great option.

• **Chalk.** Tailor's chalk is very useful for marking a design, whether it's for cutting, sewing two-of-a-kind HST blocks, centering a motif, or anything else. You can also use the same fabric marker from your embroidery kit, if you prefer.

• **Bias/binding tape maker for 2-in. strips.** I love to make my own binding for quilts and minis, and it's also useful for nicely finishing any kind of edge. I use a Clover 25 bias tape maker, which turns 1⅞-in. or 2-in. strips of any medium-weight fabric into perfect custom double-fold binding.

• **Safety pins or QuilTak baster.** Basting a quilt, pillow, or anything you're going to quilt is much easier with the right tools (for more on this, see p. 53). Oversized safety pins that catch all layers of your quilt sandwich or a quick, easy baster that uses small plastic tabs like those found on price tags in a store are both great beginner-friendly ways to go.

• **Zip-top bags in quart and gallon sizes.** These bags are useful for collecting scraps or keeping everything that goes with projects in progress in one place.

• **Post-it Notes or paper squares.** Using these small paper squares is one of the simplest and easiest (and certainly cheapest) ways to keep your quilt blocks layout organized as you assemble a top. Just number your notes and pin them to the upper left corner of each leftmost block, then make stacks of each row, working from left to right.

document the story of your quilt

Each of my quilts and patchwork projects tells a story, whether it's published in one of my books or is a special gift for someone. I like to keep my own record of what techniques I used, what turned out to be the easiest method or the nicest finish, how I chose my colors or prints, or what inspired me in the first place. I started keeping these sewing journals more than 10 years ago, and it's so much fun to page through them and remember details that would have slipped away otherwise. Here is what I use:

• **Blank journal.** For every project, I date my entries, make notes, swatch fabrics, note measurements or alternative ideas, write down tips . . . it's like a diary of my sewing. I also keep running lists of what I need the next time I go to the fabric store, jot down new ideas, or do my binding math so everything is in one place. I always use a good-sized spiral-bound journal made from recycled vintage books.

• **Good pencils.** I love my Staedtler Mars Lumograph pencils for neat, clean lines for sketching or writing, and I have a Pink Pearl eraser and a little sharpener nearby. But a regular mechanical pencil that never dulls is great, too!

• **Stapler.** I include swatches of fabric in my journal, and stapling in fabrics will ensure they stay put. I like to cut my fabrics at least ½ in. across—bigger if there's an interesting print motif or detail.

NICE-TO-HAVE TOOLS

Though not necessary, the following tools can help make your quilting and sewing experience more fun and less frustrating.

• **¼-in. presser foot.** This sewing-machine foot is wonderful for sewing fast, accurate ¼-in. seams in patchwork quilting. If you're more used to garment sewing with its typical ⅝-in. seam allowance, the narrower quilting seams can be harder to eyeball at first. A simple style with a ¼-in. mark at the front is very useful. (The ¼-in. foot I have also widens to ⅜ in. where it clips on.) You can use a presser foot for sewing narrow seams, but I'd recommend marking or placing tape at the ¼-in. line so you have a visual reminder.

• **Invisible zipper foot.** If you'd like to make simple, beautifully finished pillows, I recommend investing in an invisible zipper foot. (You can also make envelope-style backs, if you prefer.)

• **Pinking shears and craft scissors.** Having one or both of these handy for paper or patterns is a bonus.

• **Ruby Ruler or Sew Red Glasses or lenses.** Like a digital camera with a black-and-white filter, these special red-lens tools sharply separate fabric colors into dark and light values so you can really see how they would read in a block or a whole quilt design. Blair Stocker's Ruby Ruler doubles as a 5-in. square quilting ruler, the size of charm squares. Some colors in the red and pink families may not show their relative value as accurately, so keep that in mind.

• **Bobbin winder or prewound bobbins.** Having full bobbins in the right color and ready to go is a huge plus for sewing or quilting projects. I have a small machine called a SideWinder to wind extra bobbins without rethreading my machine, and I also buy sets of prewound bobbins in white or neutral colors to use for piecing.

• **Measuring tape.** A flexible measuring tape is also nice to have.

• **Walking foot.** A walking foot helps feed bulky fabrics (like the basted layers of a quilt sandwich) smoothly and evenly through your machine as you stitch, so everything stays neatly aligned for successful machine quilting. You can buy a special walking foot to use for your machine, but some like mine come with a built-in option like integrated dual feed (IDT), which is very handy.

take a shot

Using your phone to take photos of everything from your very first fabric pulls to your (hopefully) final block layouts is a great way to get a fresh perspective and "see" something in the design your eye may not have registered. You can also filter a snapshot to black-and-white/grayscale and get a better sense of how lights and darks are interacting within a palette or a design. And always (always!) take a last photo of the layout you're happy with, for reference. Then, if a block is flipped in your stack as you assemble a row, a quick glance back shows you exactly where it goes.

techniques

WHETHER YOU'VE SEWN PROJECTS BEFORE OR ARE AN enthusiastic beginner, here are the techniques you'll use to make everything in this book, from pretty hand embroideries to colorful bed quilts. With a bit of practice, you'll be off and running in no time!

hand-stitching + embroidery

Let's start with embroidery—hand-stitching a decorative design on fabric to elevate the simplest of pieces with deeply personal meaning, stitch by stitch. Handwork is not just wonderfully calming and meditative, but easy to take with you.

LET'S MAKE AN EMBROIDERY SAMPLER

The five basic embroidery stitches in this book— running stitch, tiny crosses, cross-stitch Xs, backstitch, and chainstitch (and its beautiful spin-off, the lazy daisy)—are the perfect palette for beginner-friendly stitching. You can use any combination of them to decorate, outline, echo, hand-quilt, personalize, and bring a project to life using perle cotton (my favorite) or six-strand embroidery floss.

To practice and learn these stitches, we'll make a beginner-friendly Sew + Quilt Embroidery Sampler. You'll get familiar with using a hoop, marking a simple design on your fabric, learning each of the stitches, and getting a sense of spacing that appeals to your eye.

Don't worry about perfection at first—just get the rhythm of stitching so it feels comfortable. After some practice, you can work on consistency, length, and staying close to the line. Part of the charm of embroidery is the tiny discrepancies and differences here and there that add personality, texture, meaning, and liveliness—seeing the maker's hand in a special project, instead of something that's consistent and "perfect." And if you don't like your stitches, simply unthread your needle, gently pull them out, and then start fresh.

Turn the page to get started!

Another Idea *from* Rebecca Ringquist of Dropcloth

Keep needles threaded. In fact, in an empty moment, thread 10 or 12. You'll be so glad you did when you sit down to work and you don't have to stop to get ready. A pincushion full of threaded embroidery needles also makes a most welcome gift for a quilter or embroiderer friend.

WHAT YOU'LL NEED

- Embroidery Kit (pp. 8–10), including a 7-in. hoop, quilt ruler, and chalk or fabric marker
- One 9-in.-square piece of quilting cotton or muslin
- One 9-in.-square piece of muslin for backing
- Perle cotton or floss in one or several colors. I used rainbow colors for fun, but choose a combination you like (such as monochromatic, alternating two shades, or working from dark to light).

PREPARE THE HOOP FOR STITCHING

1. Loosen the screw at the top hinge to open the adjustable outer hoop, and remove the inner hoop.

2. Align the cotton and muslin and press them so they're layered together flat and smooth. The embroidery surface fabric should be placed right side up—this will be the top layer that shows. The underlayer can be any light- or neutral-colored muslin.

3. Center the inner hoop under the fabrics, and guide the outer hoop over it so it clicks into place. If it's too tight, loosen the screw. Once the fabrics are neatly in place, tighten the screw until the circular sewing surface area is smooth and taut.

 HERE'S MY ADVICE

I usually like to make my embroidery and hand-quilting stitches about ¼ in. across, or in the case of Xs and tiny crosses, about ¼ in. square, so you'll see that general formula in my projects. I made my stitches a little bigger in the Embroidery Sampler since there was so much open space and I wanted more color. Use whatever size feels natural to you or you like the look of, but really large stitches are more vulnerable to being pulled out or loosening over time due to wear.

18

HERE'S MY ADVICE

The muslin underlayer is optional but it helps to ensure threads and knots don't show through to the surface fabric with your stitching; it also finishes the piece nicely.

MARK THE FABRIC

1. Place a quilt ruler over the prepared hoop, centering it vertically so the edge is straight and aligned with the screw hinge at the top and the ½-in. marks are lined up with the full measurement of the fabric inside the hoop (**a**).

2. Use a water-soluble fabric marker to make a small dot at each ½-in. interval, starting at the top and moving down. Leave the very last ½ in. unmarked, as shown. You should have 12 dots centered on your fabric.

3. Now turn the quilt ruler so it's horizontal and begin marking straight horizontal lines across the fabric, from edge to edge of the hoop frame (**b**). It's okay if a line isn't straight, lands too high or low, or veers off; just re-mark a straighter line again so it's obvious which one to follow. Mark all 12 lines, left to right, leaving the 1-in. section at the bottom unmarked.

THREAD THE NEEDLE

1. Cut a single strand of perle cotton, or one length of all of the intertwined strands of floss, about 18 in. long. If you're using floss, hold one end and carefully separate a single strand, gently pulling it free from the others. Set it aside and repeat to take out a second strand, then align them together with ends matching, creating a double-strand thickness. (I'll refer to both of these options as "thread" from now on, whether you're using a single thicker strand of perle cotton or a double strand of floss.)

2. Slip one end of the thread through the eye of a sharp embroidery needle and gently pull a tail of 4 in. to 6 in. through, leaving the majority of the length as your working thread.

3. Now tie a sturdy knot near the opposite end of the working thread.

HERE'S MY ADVICE

When you're just getting started, a knot is easiest, but for two-part stitches like Xs or backstitch, you can leave the thread tail loose and catch it with the first few stitches to secure it on the back of your embroidery.

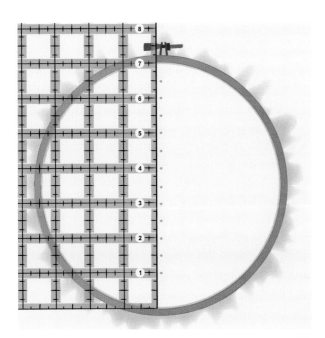
a

b

19

START STITCHING

In these instructions, we'll work from left to right to make horizontal rows of stitches, like the way we write by hand (here in the U.S.). If working from right to left feels more natural, simply reverse direction and stitch the rows your way.

RUNNING STITCH — — —

Lines 1 + 2

This is the simplest stitch by far, creating a pretty dotted-line effect. Use it to decorate or embellish rather than hold the structure of a project together. Running stitches can be straight, turn a corner, or trace along a curve; think of your first few rows as practice to get the rhythm of spacing and length.

1. Bring the needle up through the fabric from the back (wrong side) to the front (right side), settling your knot in place at the left end of the top line you've marked.

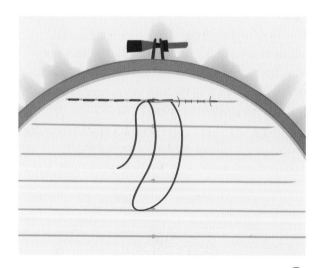

(a)

2. Now sew a forward row of stitches, following the marked line (**a**). You can either dip the needle in to form a single stitch, then pull the thread until the stitch lies flat, or create a line of three or four stitches all at once on your needle, as shown, and then pull the thread through (gently!) to fill them. Try to keep your stitch length and spacing between stitches fairly consistent as you go.

HERE'S MY ADVICE

When I say "settle" the knot on the wrong side of the fabric, I mean gently tug the thread until the tension of the thread is taut but isn't being pulled too tight or hanging loose. Too tight, and you risk puckering the fabric or, worse, pulling the knot through; not tight enough and you'll end up with loose stitches.

3. When you reach the end of this row, drop down to make another row on the marked line just below it, working in the opposite direction this time to double back. Knot when you are finished with the last stitch or if the thread runs out. If you don't like the stitches when you're finished, just snip the thread and pull it out to start again.

TINY CROSS + + +

Lines 3 + 4

This takes the horizontal running stitch a bit further, adding a vertical stitch to form a small cross. You'll first make a straight row of running stitches, working from left to right and making a secure knot as you would for running stitch. Then, double back at the end of the row of stitches and start to transform them into crosses, working from right to left.

1. Fill the third marked line with horizontal running stitches, made the same way as the two rows above. Stitch one row of running stitches and finish with the needle and thread at the back of your work.

2. Now look at the last stitch in the row you just finished, and mark (or eyeball) its center. Bring the needle through from the wrong side to the right side, just above the midpoint of the last running stitch. Make a single perpendicular vertical stitch that starts *above* and finishes below the running stitch to form a two-part and relatively symmetrical cross (**a, facing page at top**). The marked line on the fabric will become the midpoint of the vertical stitch, so keep the length of the cross part of the stitch consistent as you stitch.

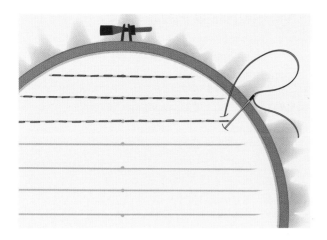

a

HERE'S MY ADVICE

For neater tiny crosses, as you make your vertical stitches, slide the needle under the running stitch so it's between the stitch and the right side of the fabric, instead of over it, then continue as usual. This way, the vertical stitch is tucked under the first finished stitch, and the entire cross stays in place flatter. Whichever method you choose is totally up to you. Just be sure to follow one method as you form the stitches. This also works nicely for Xs.

3. Move left to the next stitch in the row, and bring the needle over to start *below* the center of the stitch (**b**). Finish the stitch upward, to form a second cross, then move to the third stitch from the end.

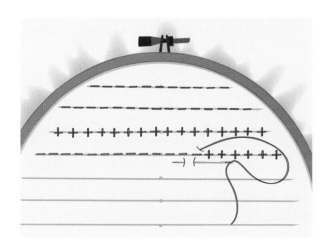

b

X/CROSS-STITCH

Lines 5 + 6

You may have tried counted cross-stitch on gridded fabric, a great template for making small, identical Xs as part of a larger pixelated design. In hand-stitching on woven fabric, you'll make similar Xs, but space them more organically along a line rather than place them so precisely.

I like to make my Xs a similar size to my crosses, also using the marked horizontal line as my midpoint reference.

1. Starting on the fifth marked line, just below the tiny crosses, form a diagonal stitch by bringing the needle up from the back of the fabric at the upper left, above the marked line, then inserting it at lower right, below the line (**a**).

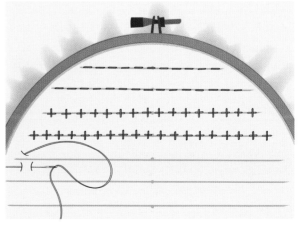

a

21

2. Finish the X with a second diagonal stitch, working from lower left to upper right. These two stitches form the first X, which also sets the scale for the rest of the row. (If you like, bring the second stitch up under the first, as in the tip for making neater crosses.)

3. Repeat to finish two lines of Xs (**b**). I like to save thread by moving from the upper right of one X to the upper left for the next X (as shown), so there's just a small stitch on the back rather than a big diagonal. Experiment to see what is most comfortable for you.

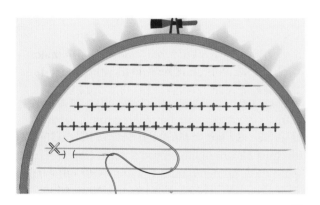

b

BACKSTITCH ─ ─ ─
Lines 7 + 8
This workhorse stitch is not only secure and sturdy but also makes a clean, continuous, and beautiful line for everything from bold outlines to handwritten letters and fancy flourishes.

1. To start the backstitch, make one running stitch forward (from left to right) at the beginning of the seventh marked line, pulling the thread through until the knot rests against the back of your fabric. Then, bring the needle back up through the fabric one stitch length ahead of where you finished the first one (**a**).

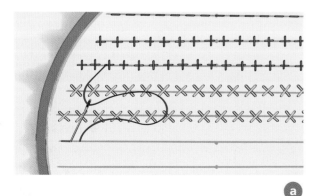

a

2. Now, bring the needle *back*—working from right to left—to meet the end of the first stitch, so that the second one joins it continuously (**b**), rather than forming two distinct stitches (like the dotted-line running stitch). Try to pass the needle through the exact hole the previous stitch ended with for the neatest results.

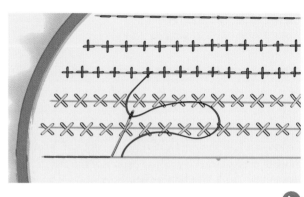

b

3. Repeat to bring the needle up again ahead of the first two stitches, then back down to meet the second stitch's end.

4. Continue stitching in this way, working your way across the marked line until you reach the end, and then drop down to backstitch the next line, working in the opposite direction. You'll notice as you backstitch that the right side of your embroidery looks like a single, neat line with no breaks, but the underside will show your working thread doubling back—you're creating a very sturdy stitch that's reinforced.

CHAINSTITCH ∞∞
Lines 9 + 10
This lovely decorative stitch is made up of a series of loops, either arranged in a row or radiating out from a single center like the petals of a flower.

1. Begin by bringing the needle through from the wrong side to the right side at the beginning of the ninth marked line; pull the length of working thread through, so the knot is secure against the back of your stitching. Now bring the needle back down through the same hole, leaving your working thread as a big loop on the right side—do not pull it back through right away (if you accidentally do this, it will all disappear; just start the stitch again).

2. With the thread loop resting on the fabric surface, bring your needle from the wrong side to the right side again, one stitch length ahead of the first hole, and begin to pull the thread through. Before the loop starts shrinking, pass your needle up through the loop so it's caught securely (**a**), then continue pulling the thread until the loop flattens against the fabric. Don't pull too hard, or the thread will look like two tight parallel lines; the loop should have a little openness to it, so it curves like the link of a chain.

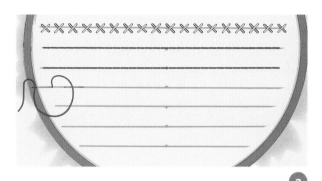

3. Make a second chainstitch the same way, bringing the needle back through the second hole, catching the loop a stitch length ahead, and so on (**b**). Finish at the end of the row by catching the final loop, tightening it to lie flat, and then securing it with a tiny stitch to complete it.

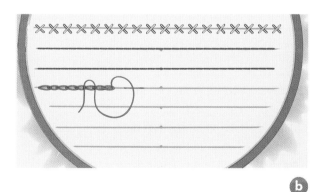

4. For your second row of chain stitches, you can either knot at the back and cut the thread to start, working again from left to right, or simply drop down to the next row, stitching with the same working thread to double back. To finish, secure your last chain loop of the row with a single tiny stitch, then knot at the back (**c**).

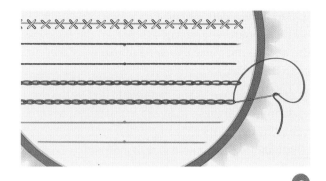

LAZY DAISIES
Lines 11 + 12

Lazy daisies are a lot of fun to make! I like to make mine a bit freeform, rather than identical each time, and use five or six "petals" in each so they're not crowded.

1. To begin, use the marked line as the flower center, making sure you have plenty of space above and below, as this stitch grows in all directions rather than forming a straight line. Bring the needle from the wrong side to the right side about ⅓ in. over from the start of the 11th line, and settle a knot at the back of your fabric.

2. Create a first chainstitch in the usual way, but stitch upward rather than to the right for a line of stitches. Catch the loop and secure it with a tiny stitch as you would to finish a row of chainstitches (**a**). This is your first petal.

3. Now bring your needle back up through the center hole again, and radiate a second chainstitch outward in the opposite direction from the first—either exactly across for an even four- or six-petal flower or at a slight angle for an odd number like five or seven petals. I like to make five for my daisies, so that's what you'll see in my sampler.

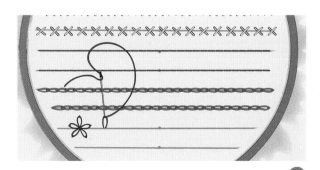

4. Secure the second petal loop with another tiny stitch. Now fill in the rest of the "petals" the same way, moving around the whole circular area to radiate out from the center.

5. Space your next flower generously (I placed my centers about ¾ in. apart on the marked line) when you're making a row of them, so the petals don't overlap. Lazy daisies tend to take up about twice as much space as a typical stitch.

6. For my second row, I stitched the same way, offsetting my daisies so they fit in between the ones above, then went back through both rows and added a tiny running stitch between each one, to connect them with a little motif.

SIGN AND FINISH YOUR SAMPLER

To finish your Sew + Quilt Embroidery Sampler, use the small open space at the bottom of your work to sign and date it.

1. Write in your name and the year, if you like, with a water-soluble fabric marker.

2. Outline the letters and numbers with a backstitch. I also added a running stitch and tiny cross on either side of my name and date.

3. Make sure all threads are trimmed, then loosen the hoop hinge and take out your work. Remove all fabric markings, like dots and lines, following product directions. If you are using a water-soluble fabric marker, be sure to soak the fabric with cool distilled water until all marks are gone. Let it dry on a folded towel, out of direct sunlight.

4. Press the embroidered piece under a pressing cloth with a warm iron, then put it back in the hoop and tighten the hinge to hold it in place.

MACHINE-SEWING

Once you've gotten some practice with hand-stitching and embroidery, machine-sewing is a perfect next step. If you're new to sewing with a machine, you'll find some great beginner-friendly book recommendations in Resources (p. 153). Sewing-machine dealers and fabric shops often offer basic classes to help you get to know your machine, or, like me, you may be lucky enough to have a friend show you how to get started!

BEFORE YOU SEW

Before you sew, or even turn on your machine, you need to cut and press your fabric. Taking care with this will make a beautiful difference in your finished piece, whether it's a tote bag, a bed quilt, or anything in between.

Press

Pressing your fabric at the beginning of a project and as you work is crucial, whether you're working with yardage, precuts, or scraps.

1. Set your iron to the correct setting ("cotton" for quilting cotton or 100% cotton denim, "wool" for wool fabrics of any weight, "blend" for a fabric of mixed content, "linen" for linens or heavily linen blends, and so on). If in doubt, always use a lower setting to get started, and test both your iron setting and any distilled water or light spray starch you'll use on scraps of fabric or by a selvage.

finger-pressing

You can often finger-press seams as you piece patchwork blocks—instead of stopping to get up and iron them every time, just smooth and flatten the seam in the right direction, then continue your sewing. When you finish the entire block, press both the wrong and right sides with the iron as usual.

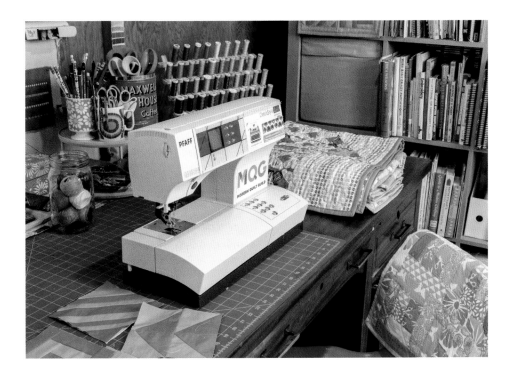

2. Press the fabric with the grain, moving your iron smoothly over the surface rather than pressing it firmly, which can distort the fibers and push them out of their woven pattern. Always use steam or spray water when pressing wool; many cottons and linens do well with light spray starch or water. These liquids can help remove creases and wrinkles by relaxing the fabrics' fibers. A dry iron can scorch some fabrics, particularly wool.

Measure + cut

Measuring and cutting your pressed fabric comes next.

1. Carefully measure the dimensions you need to cut, using a quilting ruler for straight lines or marking off measurements with chalk if you're using scissors, and then double-check them. Measure twice, cut once! If you do make a mistake, just start again with fresh fabric.

2. To use scissors, begin at one edge of your fabric, carefully following your marked line and pausing to turn any corners. Sharp fabric shears can cut virtually any weight of fabric, but to minimize distortion or fabric shifting, I recommend cutting one layer at a time.

3. To cut with a rotary cutter, place your pressed fabric on a cutting mat. Align your quilt ruler over the fabric and check to make sure the grainline is parallel to the marked grid of both the mat and the ruler. If you're cutting strips the WOF (width of fabric), arrange your fabric with the fold near you and the selvage edges at the opposite end of the mat. Square up your fabric edges if need be (see p. 26). Then place your quilt ruler over the folded fabric, aligning it so it covers exactly the width of the strip you want to cut (in this example, a strip 2 in. wide from selvage to selvage). You will use the rotary cutter with your dominant hand while holding the quilting ruler in place with the other (**a**). (Note: These illustrations show how I cut my fabric as a right-handed person; if you're left-handed, you may want to align your fabric and quilt ruler in the opposite orientation.)

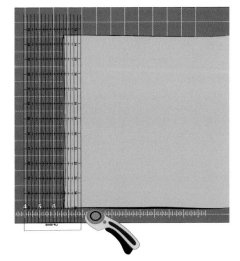

4. Holding the quilting ruler in place, and with a firm grip on the handle of the rotary cutter, smoothly cut in a straight line, away from your body and following the edge of the quilting ruler exactly, from the fold to the selvage edges. Use firm, even pressure, and *always* close and lock your rotary cutter before setting it down.

5. To cut additional WOF strips, lift the ruler, move the first strip to the side, realign your ruler over the fabric at the measurement you want, and cut the next strip the same way (**b**). Remember, always close and lock your rotary cutter, and store it and your scissors well away from fabrics and materials (and any children or pets).

SEWING CONSTRUCTION
Basic seams

To transform pieces of plain, flat fabric into a quilt block or three-dimensional project, you'll sew straight seams with a consistent seam allowance. This gets much easier with practice, as your eyes get used to instantly recognizing the measurements called for (¼ in. for patchwork and piecing, ½ in. for many of the sewing projects in this book). Let's practice using both seam allowances on quilting cotton.

1. Cut two 3-in. squares of fabric A and two of fabric B. Pair one square of A with one of B, right sides facing and edges matching. Pin or hold in place.

2. Mark or eyeball your ¼-in. seam allowance (the distance from your stitch line to the raw edges of the fabrics). You will sew along this line to join the layers together (**a**).

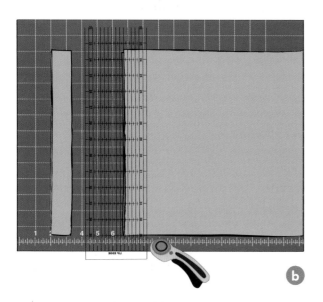

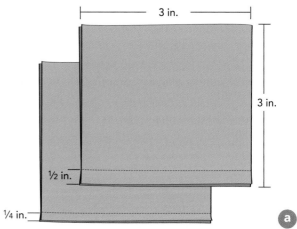

squaring up and cutting on grain

Fabrics are woven so that the threads are neat and straight and the weave is at a perfect 90-degree angle in both directions. The *cross-grain* runs across a fabric's width, from selvage to selvage, and the *grainline* runs perpendicular, the length of the fabric. You'll notice that if you gently tug fabric across either of the grainlines, it is firm and taut, but if you tug a piece of fabric at a 45-degree angle, it stretches much more. This is called the *bias*.

If you cut your strips or squares carelessly so the edges aren't straight, the fabric will not press, sew, or lie as evenly, since the bias can distort or stretch much more easily. Square up your fabric (trim away any wavy or uneven edge just slightly, so it's neat, straight, and on grain) before cutting strips in the same way you'll square up the edges of your pieced quilt blocks a little later on.

3. Sew two or three stitches, then reverse to backstitch, which secures your stitching just as tying a knot would. (In some patchwork, like log cabin or string blocks, you don't need to backstitch at the beginning or the end, since your next round of piecing will cover the earlier stitching, but let's use it in this practice piece.) Continue stitching forward, making sure your seam allowance is neat and straight. If you veer or curve, or if your fabrics are out of alignment, just seam-rip that section and resew it.

4. End with a few stitches of backstitching for sewing projects or without it for piecing.

5. Repeat these steps with your second pair of fabric squares, using a wider ½-in. seam allowance this time.

6. Press both sets of your joined fabrics, first on the wrong side (back) (**b**) and then on the right side (front). For many of the quilt blocks, I recommend pressing both seams to one side (for example, away from the center in log cabin or toward the darker side in HST). In a few specific projects, pressing your seams open works better. Look for the suggestions offered with each project. As you'll see here, the width of the seam allowance disappears when you join fabrics together, leaving your finished piece ½ in. smaller if you use a ¼-in. seam allowance or 1 in. smaller if you use a ½-in. seam allowance.

5½ in.   5 in.   **b**

Topstitching

Topstitching adds crisp definition and sturdiness to a sewing or patchwork project, as well as a decorative element if you use a contrasting thread color (like the back pockets of jeans). I used topstitching on all the block seams in my denim Basketweave Picnic Quilt (p. 94), as well as my wool Courthouse Steps Housewarming Quilt (p. 148) and Mt. Hood Memento Quilt (p. 116).

1. Press both seams to one side on the wrong side (back) of the piece, and then turn your project over so the right side is facing up to press along the seam again. Pin the seams in place if you're using a heavier fabric like wool or denim, and set your stitch length to longer than usual since you'll be sewing through four layers instead of two.

2. Start topstitching at one edge of a block or project, about ⅛ in. to one side of the seamline, stitching through all layers of fabric and catching the pressed seams at the back. Sew parallel to the seamline so your topstitching is neat and straight; if it wavers or veers, just seam-rip the stitches and start again.

3. Sewing all around the perimeter or opening of a project (like my Sashiko Drawstring Bag on p. 68), is called edgestitching, simply meaning that you are topstitching along an edge rather than parallel to an internal seam in the project.

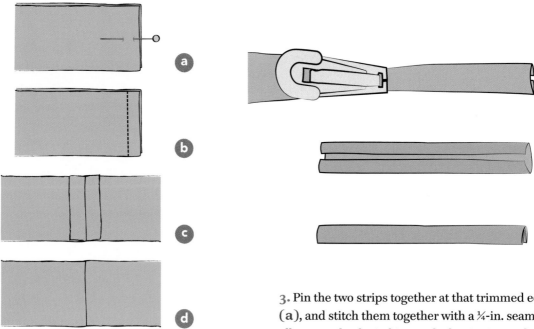

Make your own binding tape

I love to make my own binding tape, which adds a beautiful finish to sewing and patchwork projects. Whether you're edging an envelope pillow back or binding a full-sized quilt, you can cut, press, and fold any medium-weight cotton fabric, print or solid, into binding tape for a contrasting or matching finish. Note: You can also buy packages of premade double-fold bias tape (usually in solid colors) at a fabric store instead of making your own. Bias tape is designed to stretch, so it's ideal to use on curved garments or rounded edges, but you can also use it to bind quilts or along straight edges.

1. To make ½-in. double-folded binding tape, which is what I use to bind my quilts or edge the envelope back on a pillow, you'll press and cut 2-in. strips of fabric on grain to the length you need plus an inch or two extra—shorter pieces can be cut individually. If you're making longer binding (for a quilt or larger project), it's easiest to cut it on the cross grain from selvage to selvage, using a quilt ruler and rotary cutter.

2. To join more than one strip of fabric together, place two strips right sides together, matching the short ends. Trim any selvages.

3. Pin the two strips together at that trimmed edge (a), and stitch them together with a ¼-in. seam allowance, backstitching at the beginning and end to hold the seam (b). Press the seam open (c, d). You can join multiple strips the same way. Press your continuous strip once it's completed.

4. Snip one end of your fabric strip at an angle and use a straight pin or seam ripper to guide it through a bias tape maker, so the two sides are evenly feeding into it (e).

5. Pull the fabric strip through the binding tape maker, pressing it with an iron to create folded tape, with the raw long edges of the fabric pressed toward the center of the strip (f). If any tape gets uneven or out of alignment, simply dampen that section by spraying it with distilled water, easing it back through the binding tape maker, and refolding it, pressing it as you go.

6. When you reach any joined seams, you may need to carefully ease the extra layers through the binding tape maker, then continue pressing and folding.

7. After creating your folded 1-in. binding tape, fold it again in half lengthwise to create ½-in.-wide double-folded binding tape and press with an iron, moving along the length of the tape, to make a neat, straight center fold with the raw edges of the fabric hidden deep inside (g). You can wind this finished binding tape around a piece of cardstock, or simply store it in a zip-top plastic bag.

FINISHING PILLOWS

I love to make hand-quilted and patchwork pillows!
Here are two ways to finish them nicely—with an
envelope back or an invisible zipper.

Envelope back

Edge an envelope back closure with binding tape,
using either the same fabric as the back panels or
a pretty contrasting one. You can also finish the
outer panel with a second double-folded hem if you
prefer.

1. Cut two backing panels—an underlayer and an
overlayer. The underlayer should measure the same
height as the pillow front panel and half its width. The
overlayer should measure the height of the front and
approximately two-thirds its width, so there is some
overlap when it's complete.

2. For the underlayer, fold and press ⅛ in. to the
wrong side of the backing panel, then fold and press
again. Sew this double-fold section to finish the edge
(this side will not be seen from the back of the pillow).

3. For the overlayer, pin binding tape over the right
side of the vertical edge, and stitch the binding
securely near the folded edge. See pp. 47–49 for more
tips for sewing on binding. (You can also repeat step 2
to make a second simple hem.)

4. Place the pillow front panel on a work surface,
right side up. Place the overlayer back panel over it as
shown, right sides facing, and matching corners and
edges on the right side, top, and bottom. Pin in place
(a) and stitch around the three pinned sides, using
a ½-in. seam allowance and stopping to turn at each
corner 90 degrees. Backstitch at the beginning and
end of your joining seam.

5. Now place the underlayer over the other two layers
with the right side down. Align it with the left side of
the pillow front panel, so it's overlapping the binding
edge by several inches. Pin around the perimeter,
making sure the overlapped area is securely pinned,
neat and flat (b).

6. Stitch the perimeter of the pinned panel edges
using a ½-in. seam allowance. Clip corners (b), turn
your pillow cover right side out, and put a pillow form
inside (c).

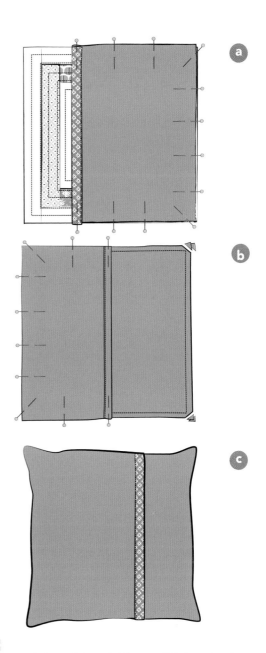

clipping corners

To finish bags, pillows, needle books, or anything
else that is turned right side out with square
corners, you'll want to clip corners before
turning. Simply snip a triangle of the excess
fabric away, being careful not to cut close to the
seam. You just want to reduce the inside fabric
bulk here so when you turn your project to right
side out, the corner opens up neatly.

Invisible zippers

These provide a beautiful, clean finish for pillows. Katie Pedersen of the quilting blog SewKatieDid graciously gave me permission to share her instructions, which I've adapted for beginners.

1. Square up your completed pillow front so it measures 1 in. larger than the pillow form, and stitch the perimeter to join all layers. Cut a back piece the same size as the front so you have two panels and choose an invisible zipper a few inches shorter than the panels measure.

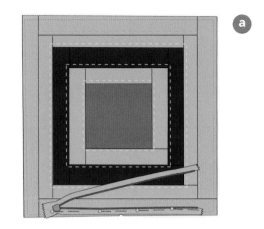

2. Measure, fold, and mark the center of an invisible zipper by snipping a tiny triangular notch with scissors. Also mark the bottom center of each of your two pillow panels with a tiny notch.

3. Open the zipper and place the lower half of it along the bottom of the right side of the pillow front panel, matching notches exactly. Pin in place as shown (**a**).

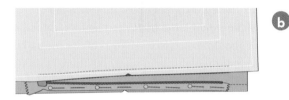

4. Using an invisible zipper foot on your sewing machine, stitch the zipper down, working from the open end to the zipper pull and backstitching to hold the seam.

5. Match, pin, and stitch the other half of the zipper to the right side of the back panel in the same way (**b**).

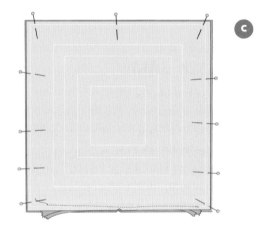

6. Leaving the zipper at least two-thirds of the way unzipped, align the two pillow panels together, right sides facing and matching edges and corners. Pin around the three open sides of the pillow, extending the zipper ends outside of the pinned section so they'll be tucked away inside the finished pillow cover (**c**).

7. Stitch from one end of the zipper all the way around the perimeter to the other, using a ½-in. seam allowance, turning each corner with a right angle, and backstitching at the beginning and end.

8. Clip corners and gently turn your pillow cover right side out. Tuck your pillow form inside and zip it up.

patchwork + quilting

LET'S MAKE A PATCHWORK SAMPLER

My four favorite quilt blocks for beginners are the log cabin, rail fence, string, and half-square triangle, so I designed a simple "practice" set of each of them as a Sew + Quilt Patchwork Sampler—a pretty mini-quilt. After you've cut your fabric, pieced each block, and finished your mini-quilt with sashing, borders, quilting, and binding, you'll have something very special to show for it—plus you'll be ready to take on any of the other quilts in the book! You can finish your sampler as a pillow cover or keep adding to it to grow it into a bigger project, if you prefer.

Here are a few things to keep in mind:

- You'll cut a mix of strips and squares to start with in two different fabrics and then use those to build all four blocks, as well as assemble and finish your mini-quilt.
- I used solids, which are easiest for a beginner, but you can use small-scale, non-directional prints if you'd like. The fabrics can be within the same color family, or very different from one another—dark and light can be very relative! I chose two Michael Miller Cotton Couture solids, Luna and Turquoise.

- You will always use a ¼-in. seam allowance for piecing these blocks (as well as adding the sashing and borders) and always sew your fabric strips and squares with right sides facing.
- Each of these mini-blocks will measure 5½ in. square when they're pieced and squared up, and then finish at 5 in. square within the quilt.

WHAT YOU'LL NEED

For the sampler blocks and mini-quilt, you'll need a Sewing + Quilting Kit (pp. 10–13).

- Choose two quilting cottons—¼ yd. of a dark color (A) and ⅛ yd. of a light/contrast color (B). I recommend buying an extra ¼ yd. of each if you're new to sewing and piecing, so you don't have to worry about running out of fabric if your cuts or stitching are off the first time.
- You'll also need a 15-in. square of batting, a 15-in. square of quilting cotton for the back (which can be the same as one of your A or B fabrics or different), and a 5½-in. square of plain muslin.

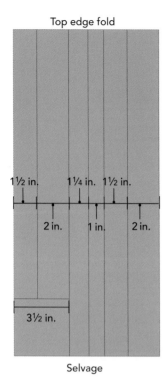

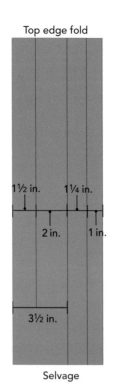

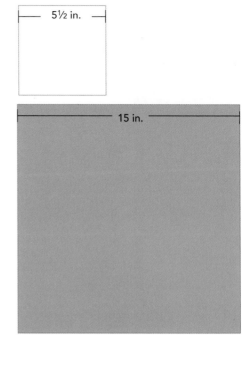

CUTTING YOUR FABRIC

1. Press your dark and light fabrics, folding them at the centerline, so the selvages are aligned and straight. Use your quilting ruler and rotary cutter to trim the selvages (which are often perforated with small holes or have a contrast color or texture), from top to bottom, through both layers of the fold.

2. Now cut strips and squares from both your light and dark fabrics the same way (see the diagrams above). From the dark and light (A and B) fabrics, cut the following:

- Two 3½-in. squares at one corner
- One 1½-in. and one 2-in. strip, cut from the fold to the edge of the 3½-in. square cut
- One 1-in. and one 1¼-in. strip, cut from edge to edge (WOF)

From the light only, cut the following:

- One 2-in. and one 1½-in. strip, cut from edge to edge (WOF)

3. Press the squares and strips. Pair the same widths of dark and light strips, using a safety pin to keep them organized and together, and label them with a slip of paper noting their widths, if you'd like.

PIECING THE SAMPLER

LOG CABIN BLOCK

I love the log cabin block, which was the first patchwork I ever tried and is still my go-to all these years later! In this pattern, you piece strips clockwise around a center square, building outward.

For our very first block in the sampler, here's a fun and easy way to piece the simplest "square within a square" version, so you'll get the knack of piecing the logs to a larger center and grow a block quickly—what my friend Heather calls "snip and flip." I've also included the instructions for the traditional light and dark block piecing later on, with my favorite tips and tricks, so you can take it further in your next project.

You'll need to cut one 2-in. square from one end of your 2-in. strip of A (dark) for the center square, then gather your 1½-in. strip of B (light) and 1¼-in. strip of A for building the logs outward.

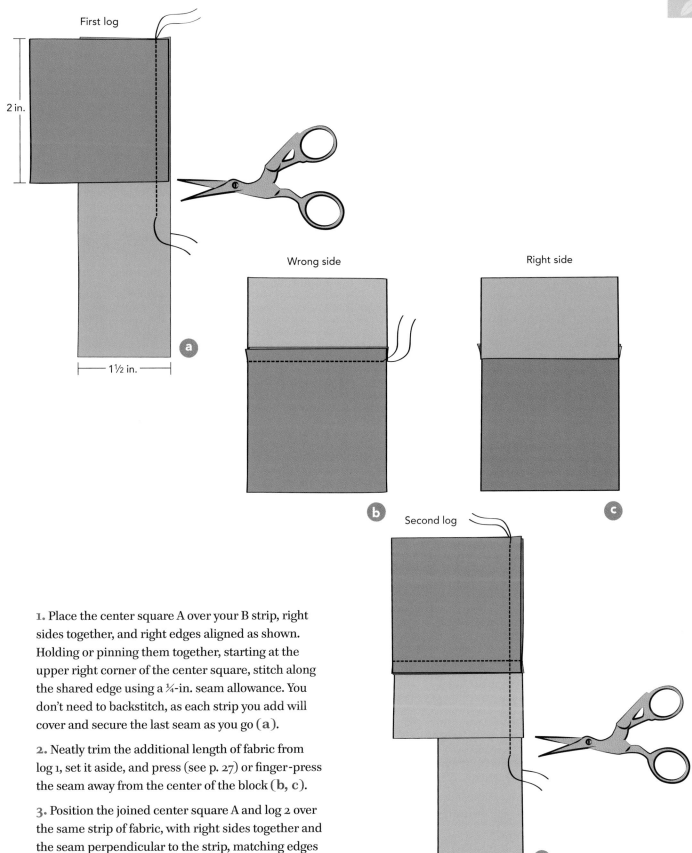

First log

2 in.

1½ in.

a

Wrong side

b

Right side

c

Second log

d

1. Place the center square A over your B strip, right sides together, and right edges aligned as shown. Holding or pinning them together, starting at the upper right corner of the center square, stitch along the shared edge using a ¼-in. seam allowance. You don't need to backstitch, as each strip you add will cover and secure the last seam as you go (a).

2. Neatly trim the additional length of fabric from log 1, set it aside, and press (see p. 27) or finger-press the seam away from the center of the block (b, c).

3. Position the joined center square A and log 2 over the same strip of fabric, with right sides together and the seam perpendicular to the strip, matching edges and ends. Join these the same way as before (d).

Trim the extra length away and press or finger-press the seam flat (**e**, **f**). Since you're piecing clockwise, that makes it easy to press the seams away from the center and easier to press the finished block as well.

4. Piece log 3 the same way, with the center square at the top right again, matching edges and ends of the center + logs to the strip, and then trim and press/finger-press (**g**, **h**, **i**).

Third log

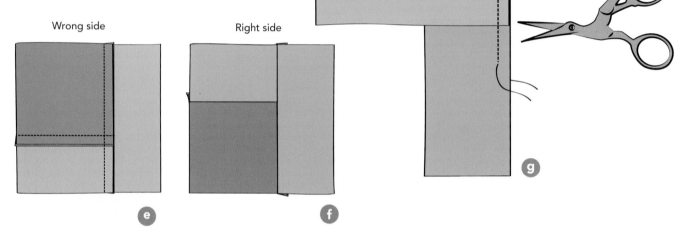

Wrong side   Right side

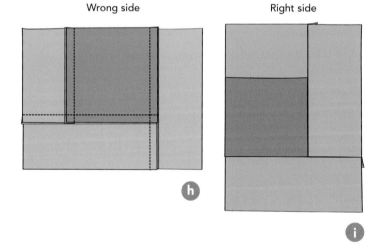

Wrong side   Right side

Fourth log

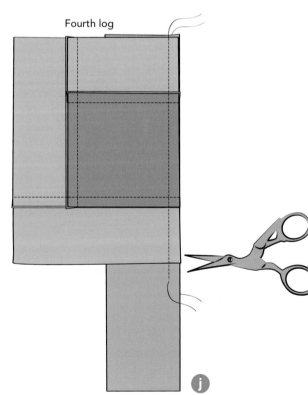

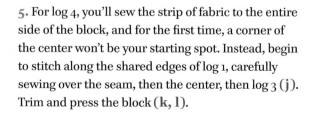

5. For log 4, you'll sew the strip of fabric to the entire side of the block, and for the first time, a corner of the center won't be your starting spot. Instead, begin to stitch along the shared edges of log 1, carefully sewing over the seam, then the center, then log 3 (**j**). Trim and press the block (**k**, **l**).

Wrong side

Right side

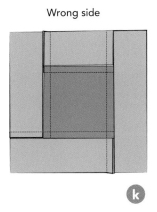
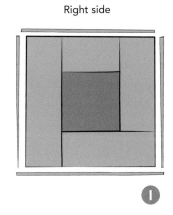

k

l

6. Now, give your block's first tier of logs a good press, first on the wrong side and then the right side, always pressing away from the center, and square up the edges of your block using a rotary cutter and quilt ruler.

7. Now you will add a second tier of logs using your 1¼-in. strip of fabric A, matching the center square. Always stitch to the shortest log in the previous tier. If you look at your current block, you'll see the shortest log—log 1—is the side where you'll begin stitching this next tier. Add logs 5, 6, 7, and 8 the same way, always working clockwise. Press and trim the edges to square them up, so your block measures 5½ in. square (**m, n**). You've finished your first log cabin block!

Block with two tiers completed

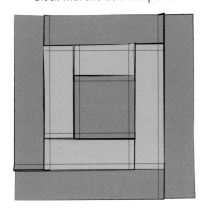

m

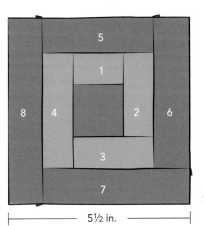

n

|← 5½ in. →|

trimming your block

You'll square up your pieced blocks by trimming each side with a rotary cutter and quilt ruler so they're even, straight, and measure the correct size. For these blocks, that's 5½ in. square.

Beyond the sampler: log cabin variations

Traditional "sunshine and shadow" log cabin quilts frequently use center squares the same width or scale as the logs—either the red or yellow symbolizing the warmth of home, or sometimes a color matching the color of the dominant logs to blend in with them in the design.

Arranging the strips so one side is "dark" and one "light" (or using just two contrasting colors) means that the finished blocks can be arranged in your choice of dazzling settings like concentric diamonds, bold diagonals, or eye-catching zigzags—with poetic American names to match.

Today, quilters not only make those traditional-style log cabin blocks but also take this versatile patchwork in many other directions, like oversized centers, offset block arrangements, unconventional colorways, wonky piecing, and more.

As you can see in the settings, the piecing technique is exactly the same, but you'd often add three (or more) tiers of logs, with their oppositional color play drawing the eye in a larger pattern in a quilt layout, rather than oversize or contrasting centers.

A courthouse steps block pairs logs of equal length on opposite sides of the center square, so instead of working clockwise, you piece two identical logs above and below the center, trim, then add the next two (longer) logs to the right and left, and so on—simple and quick to piece. This creates a strong and beautiful geometric visual but changes the overall color play since there's no "sunshine and shadow" reflective piecing.

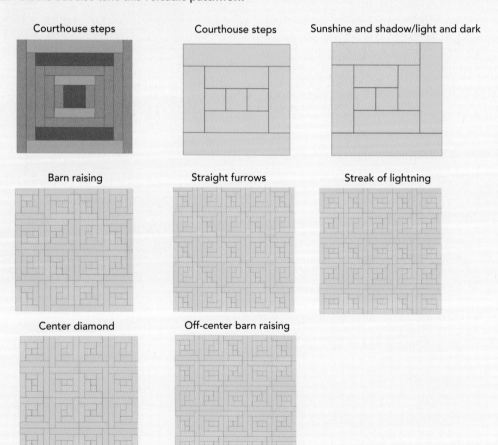

Courthouse steps   Courthouse steps   Sunshine and shadow/light and dark

Barn raising   Straight furrows   Streak of lightning

Center diamond   Off-center barn raising

Beyond the sampler: making multiples: log cabin chain-piecing

To make multiples of the same block, you can chain-piece several blocks at once, adding the same strip of fabric to grow each one and then trimming them apart again. In this example, we will chain-piece two identical 3-tier traditional blocks, all using 2-in.-wide center and strip fabrics (like the blocks in my log cabin wedding quilt on p. 132). For this example, you'll need a 2-in. by 4-in. piece of yellow center fabric, a 2-in. by 36-in. light strip, and a 2-in. by 43-in. dark strip. (Note: For log cabin piecing, you can use varying lengths rather than one continuous strip, but make sure you have some extra or can piece strips together if need be, as the logs grow longer.)

1. Place the yellow center strip over the light strip, matching ends and edges, and stitch the two layers together using a ¼-in. seam allowance. Use a rotary cutter and quilting ruler to cut the yellow center strip in half so you have two 2-in. center squares, each with a log 1 attached. Finger-press the seams away from the center (a).

2. Now place one of the center + log pairs at the end of the light strip, matching ends and edges, and stitch them as usual. When you're getting near the end of the log, slow down or stop stitching with the needle down, gently place the second pair on the strip close to the first one (not overlapping), and then stitch that one the same way, adding log 2. Trim both of these sections and finger-press the seams away from the center (b).

3. Switch to the dark strip of fabric and add log 3 in the contrast color to the two center + log pieces, one after the other, trimming and finger-pressing away from the center. Add log 4 in the dark color the same way.

4. Press your block first on the wrong side and then on the right side, with all seams pressed away from the center, and trim each edge to square it up neatly.

5. Continue chain-piecing the next tier of logs (5 and 6 with light, 7 and 8 with dark), starting with the shortest log side and always working clockwise.

6. Press the second tier of logs and square up the block as you did in step 4.

7. Add a third tier of logs (9 and 10 with light, 11 and 12 with dark), press, and trim to square up the block.

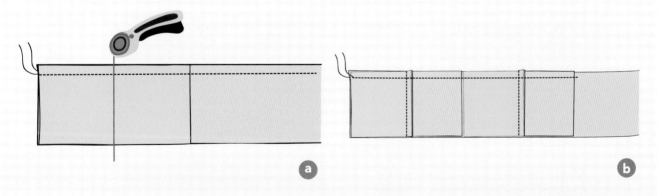

a

b

RAIL FENCE BLOCK

Rail fence is another easy block that uses all straight cutting and stitching. You simply join strips of fabric together along their long edges to create an appealing "striped" pattern.

You'll be making two of these elongated striped blocks, trimming those into four mini-blocks, and then stitching them together in a basketweave setting so the strong vertical and horizontal lines interact for lots of fun movement.

1. From each of the dark (A) and light (B) fabrics, use a rotary cutter and quilt ruler to cut two 6½-in. lengths from the 1¼-in. strips and one 6½-in. length from the 1½-in. strips, and press them. The wider (1½-in.) strip will go in between the two narrower (1¼-in.) contrast strips in this pattern (**a**).

2. Start with the set of one wider B (light) strip and two narrower A (dark) strips. Using a ¼-in. seam allowance, join one A strip to the B center along a long edge. Then join the other narrower A strip to the other long edge of B. Press both seams away from the center B on the wrong side of the block, then flip over and press the right side of the block (**b**).

3. Repeat step 2 to join two narrower B strips on either side of the A center, pressing the seams away from the center the same way (**b**). You'll now have two elongated blocks, with color placement opposite one another.

4. Use a rotary cutter and quilt ruler to cut your first long rectangular rail fence block into two identical smaller 3-in.-square blocks. First trim the left edge so it's squared up and straight. Then cut the rectangular block vertically at 3-in. intervals, and finally trim the excess away at the end of the strip. Trim the top and bottom edge of each block so all the sides of the blocks are neat and straight. Repeat with the second elongated block, so you have two sets of identical 3-in. blocks—two with dark centers and two with light (**c**).

5. Arrange them in a basketweave setting, rotating and aligning them as shown in the diagram (**d**). Pin and stitch blocks 1 (dark center, horizontal) and 2 (light center, vertical) together with a ¼-in. seam allowance to form the top row of the block, then block 3 (light, vertical) and 4 (dark, horizontal) together to form the bottom row. Press the seam joining blocks 1 and 2 to the left and blocks 3 and 4 to the right. Pin the bottom edge of 1 + 2 to the top edge of 3 + 4, nesting seams, and stitch them together. Press the wrong side and then the right side of the block, and trim it on all four sides so it measures 5½ in. square.

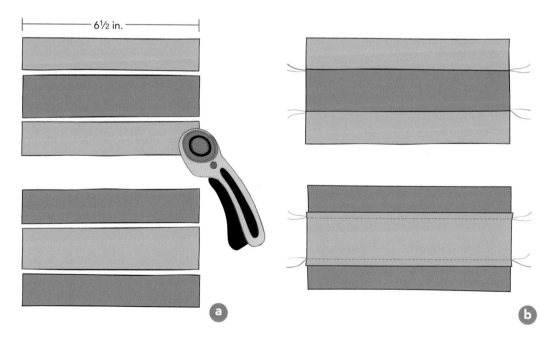

38

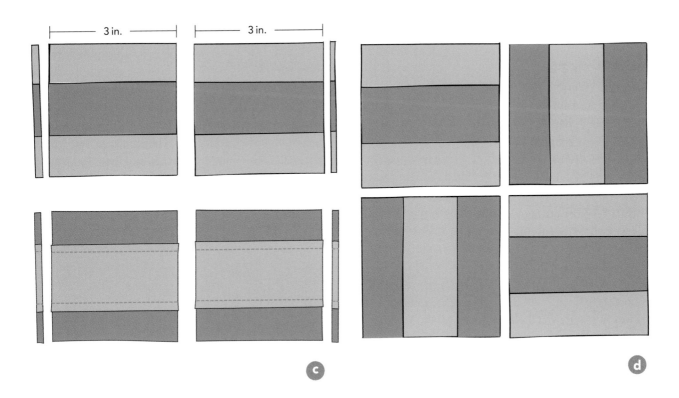

c

d

Beyond the sampler: elongated rail fence variation

Elongate the design to join generous, long strips into one giant "block." My Mt. Hood Memento Quilt (p. 116) is an example of a single rail fence block the size of a throw quilt.

Use the practice block and the elongated variation: piece long, narrow strips of fabric in threes, then trim those down to squares and set in a basketweave pattern of alternating vertical and horizontal striping, like the Basketweave Picnic Quilt on p. 94.

This super-sized version of the pattern is especially nice with the long seams pressed to one side, then secured with decorative and functional topstitching. If you're piecing long strips, just press seams to one side the whole way across, and flip the panel over to press the right side of the elongated block. Pin along the seamline and then topstitch 1/8 in. away from it, through all layers of pressed seams. This gives it beautiful cohesiveness as well as sturdy reinforcement. Then, you can trim a section into individual blocks, saving lots of time over topstitching each block one by one.

STRING BLOCK

The string block also uses straight strips of fabric, but the equally simple piecing is set on the diagonal for a beautiful, angular, and dynamic appearance. You'll foundation-piece your string blocks by stitching them onto a muslin backing that keeps the finished block from distorting its shape—and creates a very sturdy block or quilt top. Add interest to this simple design by using consistent- or varying-width strips, planning intentional placement or randomly mixing fabrics, and using colorful or monochromatic fabric choices.

For our Sew + Quilt Patchwork Sampler string block, we'll alternate the two colors, but mix in a variety of different strip widths to fill the block from corner to corner.

1. Press your 5½-in. square of muslin. Arrange one 1½-in.-wide strip of fabric A (dark) across it diagonally, extending past the opposite corners and pinning it in the center to hold it in place (a). (Note: If you're using a print fabric with a right and wrong side, the first strip is right side up.)

2. Place a second, narrower contrast strip of fabric B (light) over the first one, right sides facing, aligning them along one long raw edge as shown (b). This can be a 1¼-in. or a 1-in. strip, whichever you prefer. Stitch through all layers (two strips + muslin backing) with a ¼-in. seam allowance, following the right edge of the layered strips. Press the strips open so they lie flat on the surface of the muslin block, and trim away any excess length closer to the square's edge (do not trim it exactly; leave a bit of extra, as shown).

3. Align another strip of B fabric in a different width along the opposite long raw edge, right sides together. Stitch through all layers with a ¼-in. seam allowance, press the strips open, and trim away excess fabric (c, d).

4. Continue adding strips on both sides of the original center strip, alternating colors and randomly choosing a variety of widths, working outward until the muslin block is filled completely with fabric

strips (e). Press. (Note: If you run out of a certain width, you can trim wider strips down or cut more strips in your preferred measurement.)

5. Flip the block over so you are looking at the wrong (muslin) side (f). Use a rotary cutter and a quilt ruler or square template to precisely trim off the excess fabric on all four sides of the muslin backing so it measures 5½ in. square and is neatly squared up (g). Make sure you trim to the correct size, but don't worry if your muslin square shrinks a bit from all the stitching and pressing—any small differences will disappear when you piece the string block into the quilt.

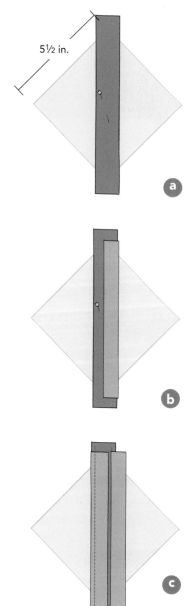

5½ in.

d

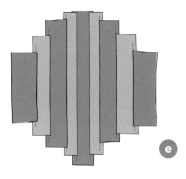

e

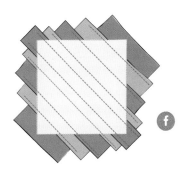

f

g

Beyond the sampler: string block variations

When you set four (or more) blocks together, you can try out all kinds of settings and arrangements. If you piece four string blocks exactly the same way, using the same placement and order of strips, you can arrange them as a striking diamond or a bold X. Mix things up with random placement in blocks, and orient four of them the same way to create dynamic diagonal movement sweeping across the quilt.

When you're making lots of the same-size blocks with consistent-width strips, you may start to notice that some designs end up almost but not quite making it to the far corners. Piecing so many 8-in. blocks with roll-up strips (2½ in. wide for Floating Crosses Quilt on p. 90), I realized I'd use one fewer strip each block if I started my piecing slightly off center instead of using the usual method of aligning the first strip exactly down the center of the diagonal.

In this variation, I arranged my first two strips so the first seam edge stretched corner to corner, not down the middle of the strip (see the diagram below), and with that simple placement shift, I ended up using less fabric!

HALF-SQUARE TRIANGLE (HST) BLOCK

I love half-square triangles—a dazzling way to create a beautiful, geometric, and fun quilt with so many options for playing with color! There are several methods for piecing HSTs, but my favorite is one of the simplest, which makes two identical blocks to mix and match. Pressing, stitching, and trimming accurately is key here, but the end result is well worth it! As with log cabin, your layout options are endless, and the way you pair and mix colors is entirely up to you. I used this method for piecing my 100 blocks in Bright Star Quilt (p. 126) to ensure a huge variety of colors and prints.

For our Sew + Quilt Patchwork Sampler HST block, you'll need the four 3½-in. squares you cut earlier, two of color A and two of color B, and chalk or a fabric marker.

1. Align your first two squares of fabrics A and B, right sides together, and edges matching. Use a quilt ruler and chalk or fabric marker to mark a neat diagonal line right down the center, and pin in place (a).

2. Using a scant (meaning slightly narrower than) or regular ¼-in. seam allowance, stitch a parallel seamline to one side of the marked line. Take the set of stacked squares out from the sewing machine, turn it around, and then stitch a second parallel seamline ¼ in. to the other side of the centerline (b).

3. Cut the stitched square in half using a quilt ruler and rotary cutter, exactly following the marked line between your seams but not cutting into them. You will now have two identical blocks (c).

4. Press the wrong side of each block so the seam is pressed toward the darker color fabric (d, e).

5. Trim each mini-block to 3 in. square using a rotary cutter and quilt ruler with a bias diagonal line you can align your seam with for accuracy (f, g).

6. Repeat these steps to make a second identical set of 3-in.-square HST blocks.

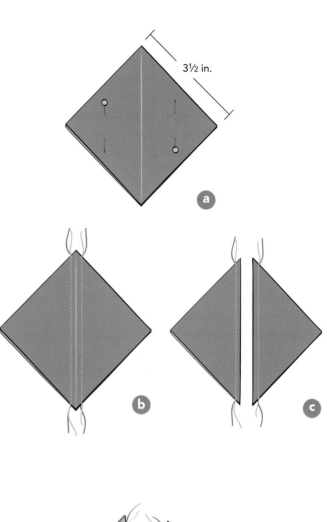

3½ in.

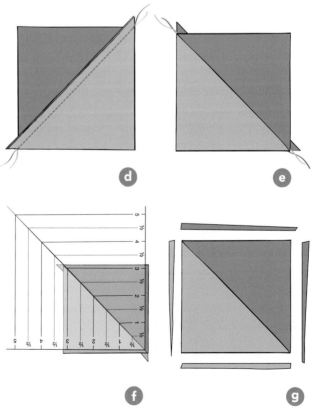

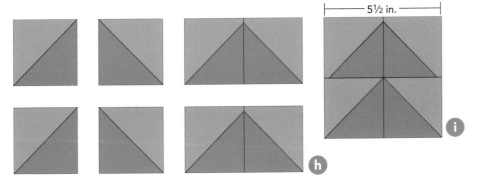

7. Arrange the 4 mini-blocks in the layout shown (**h**) (or choose your own). To make a set of flying geese as I did, pin your top-row blocks, 1 and 2, together, matching the triangle points with a pin right through the seams, and stitch with a ¼-in. seam allowance as usual. Check your point to see if the fabrics lined up, and gently seam-rip, repin, and restitch if it didn't match well. This can take a bit of practice to get right; you can also seam-rip your joining seams, press the mini-blocks, and try a new simpler setting (see below) if these points are frustrating. It really gets much easier with practice.

8. When you are happy with your triangle, press the seam open (the block will lie flat and smooth with an open seam). Join blocks 3 and 4 the same way, and press the seam open as well.

9. Pin blocks 1 + 2 to 3 + 4, matching seams and color lines. Sew with a ¼-in. seam allowance. Press the joining seam up, toward the top-row triangle, and square up your block so it measures 5½ in. on each side (**i**).

Beyond the sampler: hst variations

There are so many settings for HST blocks, including diamonds, stars, diagonals, and allover patterns. Once you have 4, 9, 12, or 24 blocks, you can create all kinds of fun layouts by rotating and rearranging the blocks. As with log cabin, some of the most exciting settings depend on mixing dark and light colors for high contrast.

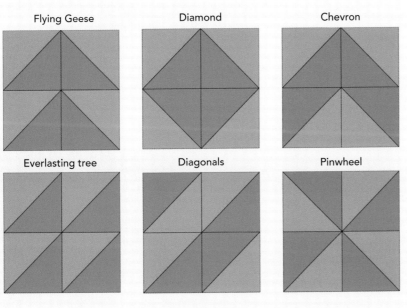

Flying Geese

Diamond

Chevron

Everlasting tree

Diagonals

Pinwheel

One thing to keep in mind when choosing fabrics for HSTs is that any directional print can get flipped or spun to a new angle, so a scatter or allover design can be more fun to work with. You'll see in my Memento Mini-Quilts on p. 112 that the crosshatch fabrics I chose for the backgrounds appear on the diagonal in regular squares, while in HSTs they are suddenly right-angle straight. Anything with words or a very specific up-down axis may be more of a challenge to place correctly.

Beyond the sampler: making multiples: 4 at a time

I love the 2-HST method for making blocks that end up a bit smaller than the original squares (for example, two 5-in. charm squares become two 4½-in. HST blocks), but if you want to make four of the same HST for a design, there's a very fun way to piece those all in one go! This is how I made my Memento Mini-Quilts (p. 112), Pinwheels Baby Quilt (p. 108), Anniversary Mini-Quilt (p. 140), and Half-Square Triangle Pinwheel Pincushion (p. 78)

For this practice version, let's start out with two 8½-in. squares of fabric, just like I used in my Pinwheels Baby Quilt, and turn them into four smaller HST blocks.

1. Press and align your fabric squares so the edges are matching and right sides are facing. Pin around the perimeter of the squares, without leaving an opening (a).

2. Starting at one corner, stitch around the squares using a ¼-in. seam allowance and turning at a right angle at each corner. Backstitch at the end of the seam to hold it securely (b).

3. Using a quilt ruler and rotary cutter, slice the squares on the diagonal as shown, bisecting each corner neatly (c). You'll now have 4 identical mini-blocks (d). Handle these carefully and press them with light spray starch, since the new "square" edges are really cut on the bias and can stretch out of shape.

4. Use your rotary cutter and quilt ruler to trim each block to 5½ in. square (e). Piece them with care so they don't stretch, pinning at center seams and color lines for a good match.

Note: When joining HST blocks, make sure you use a consistent ¼-in. seam allowance so your triangle points are neat. If you're binding an HST quilt or mini, or sewing a pillow cover with a wider seam allowance, you may want to add a 1-in. (or wider) border all around your HST patchwork so the triangle points at the edges aren't covered up. You can see an example in my Memento Mini-Quilts (p. 112).

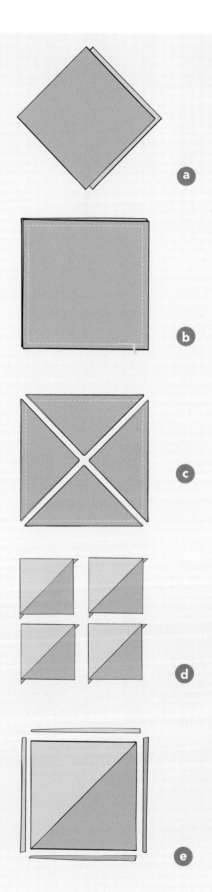

a

b

c

d

e

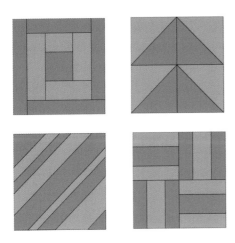

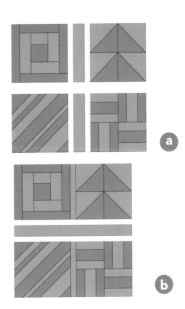

ASSEMBLING THE SAMPLER

Press the blocks and you're ready to lay out and join the rows. The sampler has two rows of two blocks, and the blocks can be positioned in the layout of your choice. This is a nice way to practice a layout on a small scale. Move the blocks around to different positions in the two rows or rotate them for new alignments and visual interest. For tips and techniques for laying out and assembling a larger quilt top, see p. 49.

Now let's sew the blocks into a mini-quilt top, using narrow 1-in. sashing and 1½-in. borders in our B (light) fabric. As with layout, working on a small scale provides a bit of practice before moving on to a larger quilt.

SASHING

Each of the four blocks measures 5½ in. square, so we'll need about 24 in. of 1-in. sashing to join them, and 50 in. of 1½-in. border strips to "frame" the blocks.

1. Join blocks 1 and 2 by stitching the right edge of block 1 to a strip of sashing, using a ¼-in. seam allowance, then trimming it flush with the block (a, above).

2. Now stitch the left edge of block 2 to the other vertical edge of the sashing strip. Press the seams towards the sashing so they lie flat.

3. Join blocks 3 and 4 with sashing the same way.

4. Sew a strip of sashing to the bottom edge of blocks 1 + 2 and trim it flush, just as you did to join the two single blocks (b).

5. Now pin the top edge of blocks 3 + 4 to the other long edge of your horizontal sashing strip, matching the block seams, and sew the same way. Press your quilt top, wrong and then right side, again pressing the new seams toward the sashing so they lie flat.

BORDERS

You'll add borders to your Sew + Quilt Patchwork Sampler the same way.

1. First, pin a 1½-in. strip of border fabric to the top edge of your mini-quilt top and stitch it on, trimming it flush at both ends (a).

2. Repeat to add a border to the bottom edge. Press both border seams toward the border and away from the center.

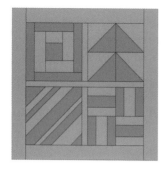

the perimeter to the corner, and then stitch back toward the center on a diagonal. Keep stitching until you reach the opposite corner, then turn to stitch to the center of that side, back to the middle, and over to the opposite side (a). Essentially, you're temporarily joining the three layers of the quilt sandwich with big, easy-to-remove stitches that form both an X of diagonal lines and a + of straight ones. See p. 53 for more tips on basting.

3. Now pin and stitch a border strip to the left side, then the right side of the quilt top, trimming them flush and pressing the new seams away from the center, toward the border (b).

4. Press and square up the edges—you've constructed a beautiful little mini-quilt top!

FINISHING THE SAMPLER

The Sew + Quilt Patchwork Sampler top now measures 13 in. x 13 in. with the sashing and borders, and once you've pressed it one last time, it's ready to add the finishing touches.

BASTING

Baste the sampler top to a 15-in. square of batting and a 15-in. square piece of backing fabric.

1. Working on a flat, clean surface, lay out the pressed quilt back, right side down. Smooth it out and, if necessary, tape the corners down to your work surface.

2. Lay your batting over the backing, centering it and smoothing out any wrinkles or creases, then place the sampler top over the batting, centering it right side up, so the batting and backing extend past the top evenly on all sides.

3. Hand-baste the sampler with a big running stitch in a contrast thread color. This is ideal for small quilts like the sampler or pillow covers and is easy to remove at the end of quilting. It also can be stitched over. Thread a needle with a contrast thread color and do not tie a knot. Starting in the center, sew a line of big running stitches up to the top edge of the quilt sandwich, leaving the thread tail hanging to the back. Making sure the quilt layers are lying flat, stitch along

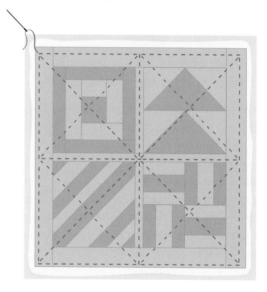

QUILTING

It's always easiest to learn a new skill when you keep things simple, so I recommend planning a basic design like straight lines or outline quilting if this is your first quilt.

For my Sew + Quilt Patchwork Sampler, I first used stitch-in-the-ditch (quilting exactly over and along the seamlines) to reinforce the joining seams on the 4-mini-block construction and my half-square triangle and rail fence block seams, which are all marked in red dotted lines on the top diagram. Then I added outline quilting—like topstitching but through all three layers—about ⅛ in. outside the seamlines, which is marked in blue, to all the other parts of my quilt, including the blocks, sashing, and borders. See the diagram on the facing page for the quilting lines and how they relate to my blocks (a).

You can also quilt in an allover pattern like horizontal straight lines (as in my Flying in Pairs mini and wall quilts), cross-hatching and diagonal patterns, or any other way you like. See p. 53 for more details on marking your quilting lines for allover patterns like these.

1. To quilt a smaller piece like a mini-quilt or pillow cover, choose your starting spot on your quilt top and adjust your stitch length to 0 or 0.5. Starting somewhere near the center and working outward is ideal. Stitch in place or backstitch for a few tiny stitches to make a secure start, almost like tying a knot. Machine-quilting is easiest with a walking foot, which keeps all the layers of your quilt sandwich moving together smoothly, but you can also use a regular presser foot.

2. Adjust your stitch length to slightly longer than usual (I like 3.0), and begin quilting forward, following the seamline or marking/tape. To turn a corner, stitch to the end of the first edge, then stop with the needle in the down position. Lift the presser or walking foot and rotate your project 90 degrees. Put the foot down and stitch forward from that point at a right angle. To end a quilting line within your design, reduce your stitch length to 0 or 0.5 again and stitch securely, using tiny stitches.

3. Work in sections of the quilt. If you're unhappy with any of your quilting or there's a fold or tuck, gently seam-rip those quilting lines, press the top and back so they are perfectly smooth, and requilt that area.

4. Continue working outward from the center until you have quilted the entire area, checking the back as you change sections to make sure it's still lying flat and smooth. When you are finished, press the top and back around the perimeter, and pin all layers securely, all the way around the edges of the quilt. Using a longer stitch length, machine-stitch the perimeter all the way around, ¼ in. from the edge of the quilt top.

5. Now square up the quilt top. Place a cutting mat under your quilt, aligning your quilt ruler with the stitched edge of the top and using your rotary cutter to carefully trim away the excess batting and backing around the perimeter stitching. Work your way around the quilt, cutting away from your body and always moving the cutting mat as you go so it's under each area you trim. You'll see your quilt shed its shaggy edges to become neat and beautiful—and ready to bind!

BINDING

I use a simple machine-binding technique I originally learned from Weeks Ringle and Bill Kerr's wonderful book *The Modern Quilt Workshop* (see Resources on p. 153) and adapted for my own quilts. It's a quick and very durable binding join, stands up to machine washing and drying well, and gets easier and easier with practice. But if you prefer another method, of course use that one instead!

To bind our Sew + Quilt Patchwork Sampler mini as a first practice piece, we'll need about 56 in. of handmade binding tape—13 in. square on each side = 52 in. of binding plus 4 in. extra. I chose to make my binding in my light (B) fabric.

1. Start binding along the middle of the bottom edge of a quilt, where the final joining seam won't be as noticeable. I like to pin my binding along the edge of the quilt on my ironing board, and often press along the folded binding sections with a warm iron to smoothly align all the layers. Fold (and press, if you like) the binding firmly around the stitched edge of the quilt so it encloses and hugs the quilt sandwich and is evenly distributed on both sides of the quilt.

2. Pin the folded binding tape to the edge of the quilt sandwich, working from the open end of the binding toward the corner of the quilt, pinning it every 2 in. to 3 in. (a); see p. 48.

3. Using a slightly longer stitch (I like 3.0), begin stitching the binding, starting about 4 in. from the beginning raw edge, and leaving that section loose for now. (This works well for a small quilt but for a larger one, you can leave 5 in. to 6 in. open.) Stitch close to the folded edge of the binding, catching all layers. Remove pins as you stitch.

4. When you get close to the corner, slow down and then stop ¼ in. from the corner, dialing your stitch length down to 0.5 and backstitching to hold the seam with "tiny stitches" (see p. 29 for more on this method). Take the quilt off the machine to check the back of the binding. If you veered off the binding on either side, you can seam-rip, press, repin, and resew it neatly, beginning and ending your new binding stitches with the same "tiny stitches" method, so the reworked stitching blends neatly with the rest of the section.

5. Now press your binding tape at the corner, making a neat triangle (**b**), and fold and press it back over the raw edge, catching and covering the end of the first seam you sewed. Pin the binding in place all the

way down the second side of the quilt. Before starting a new side of binding, hand-baste the folded corner to make sure it stays neat and crisp and doesn't shift under the machine needle (**c**). Use a bright contrasting thread, make big stitches, and don't knot. You can remove the hand-basting after you finish binding.

6. Set your stitch length to 0.5 again and stitch forward and back, starting at the corner fold, to hold the new seam securely (**d**). Adjust your stitch length back to normal and then bind the second side of the quilt. Stop stitching ¼ in. from the next corner, secure with tiny stitches, check the back of the binding, and then press, fold, and hand-baste the new corner in place.

7. Continue sewing the binding until you have stitched all four corners and are nearing the beginning raw edge of the binding. Stop stitching about 4 in. before that spot.

8. Carefully press and fold your original binding around the edge of the quilt, then overlap your new

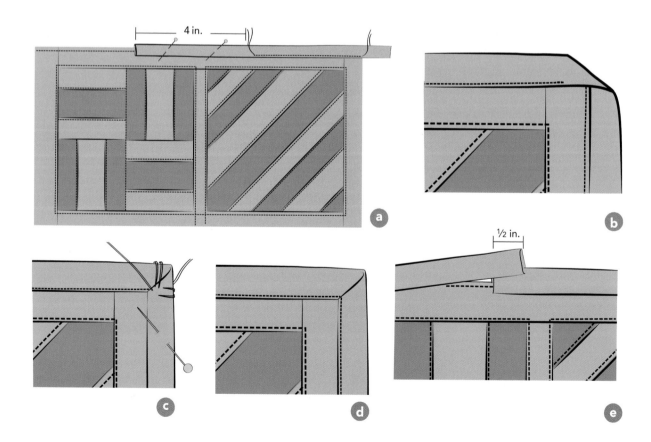

(working) binding over that. Measure ½ in. beyond the beginning raw edge of the binding, and cut your working binding to that point (e).

9. Unfold both ends of the binding, press them flat, and pin them, right sides together, short raw edges aligned. Stitch an exact ¼-in. seam to join the ends together.

10. Press the seam open, refold and re-press the binding back into place, and pin it around the edge of the quilt. It should fit snugly (f). If the binding is too loose or too tight, open the seam and adjust the seam allowance, or trim it open, stitch a new piece of binding onto the end of one strip, and redo for a perfect, snug fit.

11. Sew the last few inches of binding, backstitching at the beginning and end to secure the seam. Trim all threads and remove any basting stitches from the corners (g).

Your Sew + Quilt Patchwork Sampler is finished!

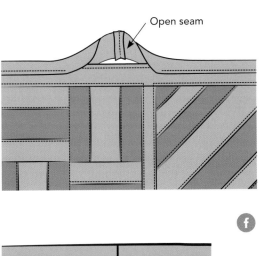

Open seam

(f)

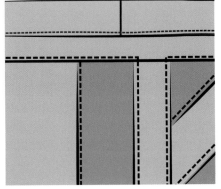

(g)

BEYOND THE SAMPLER: MAKING LARGER QUILTS

Laying out a quilt larger than two rows or two blocks is more involved. Once you've finished piecing, pressing, and trimming your blocks, the next step is choosing a layout for your quilt. This is a very personal process and can be as quick as a few block switches here or there or mixing and remixing entire sections to achieve the cohesiveness, movement, balance, and visual interest you're most excited about. There is no wrong way to lay out a quilt, but a few techniques make it easier to audition blocks.

After pressing and trimming the blocks in your quilt, arrange them on a design wall to get a good look at the entire project. This can be as simple as tacking white flannel to your wall or laying it out on a tabletop or on the floor. My sewing room doesn't have enough space for a vertical design wall, so I bring my blocks upstairs and lay them out on the living-room floor. Natural light is always a plus, but just make sure the room you're working in is well lit.

Arrange your blocks in a grid, close to each other but not overlapping. Once you have them in formation, take a photo of the layout and look at that. The camera may pick up clashing colors, "weak areas" without as much contrast or visual interest, or too-close overlaps. Filter the photo to black and white for a powerful tool in sharply defining the color values within the design. When you find places within the layout that need adjusting, don't be afraid to change blocks around. Take a photo every time you get to an arrangement that feels "better" when you look at it, and check the image to see how it reads. I probably auditioned and snapped photos of 15 to 20 layouts for my Flying in Pairs Quilt (p. 99) before it felt just right.

You can also invite a friend over to look at your block layout and give feedback, or send the progress photos to friends for their thoughts. Remember, the layout stage with raw edges showing will always look a bit less polished than a finished quilt with neatly joined blocks. Once you've decided on the final layout, it's time to assemble your quilt top.

In addition to taking photos and manually moving your blocks around, you can audition colors and layouts using a program like Quilt Canvas. Just build your quilt layout using their design tools, color sections, or blocks on the screen; rotate or change orientation, or switch colors instantly.

ASSEMBLING A LARGE QUILT TOP IN ROWS

With your layout done, it's time to assemble your quilt top! This is how I put my Pinwheels Baby Quilt (p. 108) together.

1. Count the number of horizontal rows of your quilt—in this illustration, four. Write the numbers 1–4 on Post-it Notes or small slips of paper (**a**).

2. Pin each number to the upper left corner of the first block in the row as shown (**b**). For bigger or more complex quilts, like Bright Star Quilt (p. 126), which has 100 blocks in a 10 x 10 layout, I divide the layout into quarters and mark my left and right half layout blocks accordingly—like 1A and 1B, then group each quadrant's blocks together (like 1–5A, 1–5B, 6–10A, and 6–10B).

3. Once you have labeled all rows with their numbers, take one last very clear photo for reference. This is crucial to look back at, in case your stacks get jostled or a block ends up on the floor.

4. Now you can make stacks of your blocks (and reclaim your living room or kitchen table!). Pick up all the blocks in row 1, working left to right, so the numbered block is on the top, with the others in order under it. Repeat to stack all blocks by row, and then stack all the blocks together in sequential order, from 1 to 4. Bring them to your sewing table.

5. Using the seam allowance called for, begin sewing your blocks into the rows you planned. Join row 1, working left to right, and set it aside, leaving the Post-it Note in place for reference. Continue joining rows, working from top to bottom, until rows 1, 2, 3, and 4 are each joined horizontally (**c**).

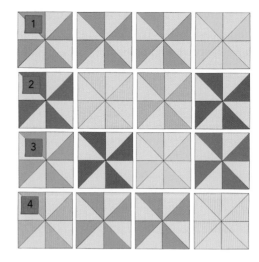

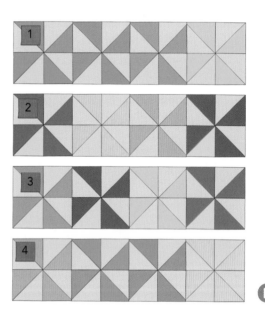

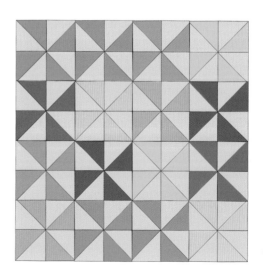

PRESSING + NESTING SEAMS TO JOIN ROWS

When you press all your block seams to the same side, you'll notice there is a lot of bulk from four layers of fabric jammed together when you join them into rows. It's much easier when you nest your seams—fit opposite-facing seams together to notch in place like a little puzzle, evenly distributing the fabric layers (**a, b**). In this example, you have four rows in your quilt top.

1. Once you've finished assembling your rows, divide them into odd (1, 3) and even (2, 4).

2. Now, press all the odd-row seams in one direction (I press them to the left), set them aside, and then press all the even ones in the other (right). It doesn't matter which one goes which way, but be consistent, so they alternate in the finished design.

3. Now, pin rows 1 and 2 together, matching seams and pinning at the seamline, with the seams nested together instead of all facing the same way. You may need to stitch over them slowly the first time, until you get the hang of it. (Note: If your Post-it Note is in the path of your joining seam, repin it in the middle of the block, but do not remove it completely.)

4. Repeat to pin, nest seams, stitch, and join rows 3 + 4, so you have two halves of your complete quilt top. Now, join 1 + 2 to 3 + 4 to complete your quilt top.

5. For a larger quilt with more rows, build your quilt top one section at a time and join those as you go. This way, you minimize the amount of accurate straight-line sewing you need to do on a heavy, unbalanced piece (for example, in a quilt with 8 rows, it's much easier to join upper and lower sections of 4 rows each at the center, rather than stitching one last row onto 7).

6. To finish a larger quilt top, carefully pin the last row join (in this example, 1–4 to 5–8), and, making sure the bulk of the quilt top is supported on your sewing table or a chair, slowly stitch the two sections together, just as you have with the others. Check the back of your quilt top to make sure all seams are straight and solid. If any of them waver too close to the edge of the fabric, carefully seam-rip those sections, pin them evenly, and sew that section again.

7. Finally, press your quilt top, first the wrong side (back) and then the right side (front) so it lies smoothly flat. I press all the row-join seams in the upper half of my quilt away from the center (upward) and the seams in the bottom half downward.

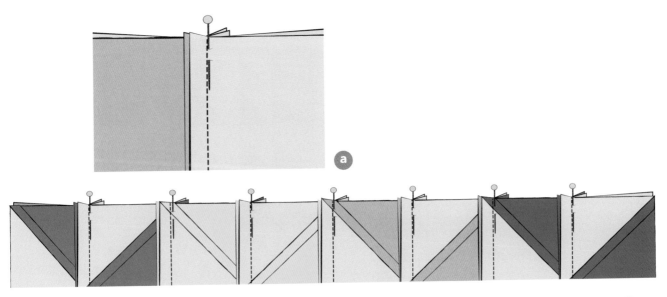

SASHING A LARGER QUILT TOP

You can also add sashing (strips of fabric between blocks or rows) as you did for the sampler instead of joining blocks directly (**a, b, c**). Sashing can calm a vibrant design, provide contrast throughout, add structure or harmony, or simply grow a finished quilt bigger without piecing more and more blocks. Here's how I assembled my Anniversary Mini-Quilt (p. 140) with narrow sashing, first joining the blocks into horizontal rows, then joining the rows together into a quilt top, always using strips of sashing the same width, then adding wider borders at all four sides to finish the quilt top (**d**). See the Sew + Quilt Patchwork Sampler sashing on pp. 45–46 for another illustrated guide.

ASSEMBLING THE QUILT SANDWICH

The next step is basting the three layers of your quilt sandwich together so they lie flat and smooth for quilting.

BACKING AND BATTING FOR QUILTING

Measure your top and add 2 in. to 3 in. to the length and width for a small top or mini, and 4 in. to the length and width for a larger top, to get the measurement for your batting—the soft middle layer of your quilt that adds dimension and loft—and backing fabric, both of which need to be larger than your top in case it shifts during quilting.

Mini-quilts can use regular yardage, cut to the correct size you need, for backs. Pillow covers or other projects that don't show the back can use plain, inexpensive muslin.

For full-size quilt backs, you can piece quilting cottons together, buy extra-wide backing fabric (which often measures 90 in. to 108 in. across), or reuse a vintage or new sheet (for more on this, see p. 6). If you're working with a longarm quilter, ask her about batting and backing dimensions.

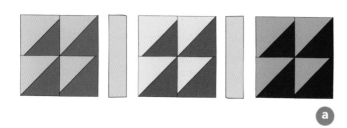

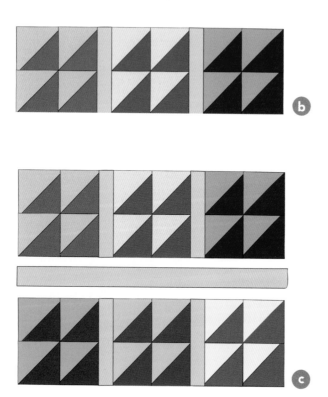

PLANNING YOUR QUILTING

Once you finish the patchwork quilt top, you can think about how to quilt it.

If you're choosing a quilting pattern that simply follows seamlines like outline quilting or stitch-in-the-ditch, you won't need to mark your top. Or if you're collaborating with a longarm quilter, you can skip both marking and basting and simply bring your pressed top and back into her studio.

Some of the simplest options are echo or outline quilting (**a**), which follows the lines of a block like topstitching; stitch-in-the-ditch, which disappears into a seamline (**b**); and geometric quilting, which can be straight lines or angles over an entire design (**b and c**). You can combine several quilting patterns in one quilt, like my Sunset Mini-Quilt on p. 106. If you're planning a more complex design, you can measure and mark your quilt top now. Use a fabric marker (always test on scraps first to make sure it comes out completely) or washi or painter's tape to lay out your quilting lines, following a ruler or using your piecing or blocks as guidelines. Once your quilt is marked, it's ready to baste!

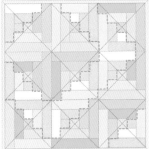

BASTING

You'll baste a large quilt similarly to the smaller sampler (see p. 46). But if you don't want to use long running stitches in a contrasting color, you have several other options for basting.

For a larger project, baste your quilt with safety pins or use a handheld quilt baster that anchors the layers together with small, flexible plastic tabs, almost like the ones that attach a price tag (**a**). Start from the center and work outward, placing pins or tabs or basting 4 in. to 6 in. apart, or closer if you like. Be sure to baste through all the layers of your quilt, and do not attach it to your living-room rug by mistake (yes, I have done this!).

I often use the plastic tabs for my larger quilts. You can quilt over or around these easily, and they're very quick to cut away after your quilting is done. If you use safety pins, you'll need to remove them if they're in the path of your quilting lines.

Many quilters spray-baste to join the layers together. Be sure to use very good ventilation if you spray-baste, and follow all the product instructions.

Now you are ready to quilt!

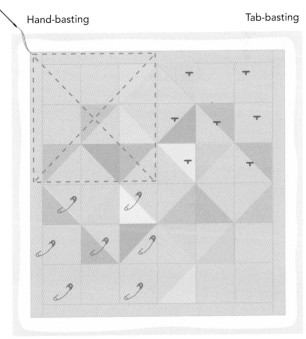

Hand-basting   Tab-basting

Safety pins   Spray-basting

how to handle all that fabric

To quilt a large piece like a throw or a bed quilt, roll it up on one side and hold it in place with a few soft-grip quilt clips. The rolled section can fit inside the "neck" of your sewing machine, and the other side can extend outward. Be sure to support the weight of your quilt on your sewing table or a chair so it doesn't pull your quilting out of alignment. You'll quilt it the same general way, but maneuvering a larger piece can be challenging, so take it slowly when shifting the weight and full width of the quilt, and don't forget to take breaks and stretch.

QUILTING

Machine-quilting

Machine-quilting is the most durable option, so it's ideal for a quilt you'll use frequently or machine-wash. You can always add hand-stitching elements as well. As I mentioned in the Sew +Quilt Patchwork Sampler steps, a walking foot makes machine-quilting go more smoothly by keeping the foot and feed dogs moving in harmony, but you can also quilt with a normal presser foot. Choose a neutral thread color for a subtle effect or a bright color to bring energy to your quilting. You may want to unspool a few feet of several colors of thread and spill them out over your quilt top to decide what color to go with!

See the step-by-step machine-quilting instructions on pp. 46–47, and work in sections, starting with the center area of your quilt, starting and ending with tiny stitches, and checking the back frequently to make sure it's smooth and even. Take breaks and stretch your hands, arms, and shoulders before moving on to the next section. Once you've gotten familiar with the basics like stitch-in-the-ditch, outline, and straight lines, you can try free-motion quilting or more complex gridded or overall designs!

Tying

For a casual or foundation-pieced design, the easiest option for finishing a quilt is tying it. You can tie by hand or machine.

To hand-tie a quilt

1. Thread a curved quilting needle with perle cotton or wool yarn, and pierce all three layers of the quilt, from the right side all the way through the layers to the back (wrong side), exactly where you want the first knot. Bring the needle back through the fabric about ¼ in. to ½ in. from the entry point, pulling your thread all the way through and leaving about a 4-in. tail.

2. Take a second stitch the same way, essentially doubling the strength of your knot, and pull the thread taut (a).

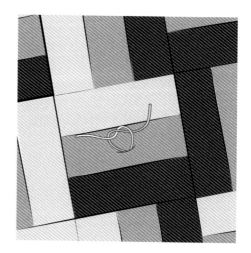

3. Trim each end of the working thread to 4 in. and make a square knot—right over left and left over right (**b**). Give the thread tails a sharp tug to make sure they are secure, and trim them to a neat ½-in. to 1-in. length.

To machine-tie a quilt

I used this approach on my Basketweave Picnic Quilt (p. 94).

1. Set your sewing machine to a zigzag stitch and adjust the length and width of the stitch to 0. Place your needle into the quilt top at the place you want to tie it, and make several stitches in place.

2. While sewing, adjust your width upward to a wide setting (do not adjust length from 0), stitch at that setting for a few seconds, then adjust the width back down to 0.

3. You can move your quilt around to machine-tie multiple spots without cutting the threads in between, if you like. I "tie" up to 10 spots before stopping, cutting, trimming my threads, and moving to a different section of the quilt.

Hand-quilting

Hand-quilting is a beautiful addition to a large quilt or mini.

Running stitches are the simplest option—whether you are hand-stitching parallel to a line of piecing in patchwork, echoing or contouring a printed or dyed design on fabric, or quilting with straight or curved lines to add a beautiful element in conversation with the fabric. They look the same on the pieced top as on the backing, so they're ideal anytime the back of the project will show, as on a quilt. They are beautiful alone, but for a quilt that will be used frequently, it's a good idea to start with sturdy machine-quilting like outline or stitch-in-the-ditch, then embellish with hand-quilting.

To hand-quilt

1. Thread a sharp needle with perle cotton or hand-quilting thread and knot the end. Bring the needle and thread through the quilt, from the backing (wrong side) up through to the surface of the quilt top, exactly where you want to start quilting, and then bury the knot by gently easing it up through the backing to hide it in the batting section, just under the fabric. (This gets easier with practice.)

2. Begin a running stitch, going through all layers of the quilt and spacing the stitches evenly. You may want to take it one stitch at a time to get the rhythm of it at first, then load two or three stitches on the needle at one time and pull the thread through. If you veer off the line you like or end up with uneven stitches, simply unthread your needle, unpick your stitches you want to redo, rethread your needle, and requilt that section. End your line of hand-quilting stitches at one edge of your quilt top, or tie a knot at the back and ease it through to hide in the batting as you did to start.

SQUARING UP + BINDING

Follow the instructions on pp. 46–49 for squaring up your quilt top, making handmade binding tape, and binding your quilt. No matter how small or large your quilt, the methods are essentially the same, and you can use premade double-fold bias tape or handmade binding tape for any of the projects in the book.

HERE'S MY ADVICE

There are so many ways to display your quilts! Visit sewplusquilt.com for some of my favorite ideas.

PART ONE

embroidery, sewing + patchwork

Now that you've learned five basic but very
useful embroidery stitches, let's make some
pretty things with them! The projects here
take the four quilt blocks you learned to
make in new directions and give you a fun
way to practice variations and mix colors
before you make a larger quilt.

Each of these projects is beginner friendly
and also offers lots of ways to customize the
details so you can make it just the way you
want to—personal, special, and fun.

Embroidery p. 58
Stitch a freeform modern sampler,
turn treasured artwork into embroidery, hand-quilt a set of beautiful
pillows in your own style, and sew a
pretty and useful sashiko project bag.

Sewing + Patchwork p. 72
Use your new patchwork piecing
skills to design and sew a set of
colorful pillows, a cheerful needle
book and pincushion set, and a
stylish tote bag. These make lovely
gifts or something special to keep
for yourself!

filled embroidery sampler

I LOVE TO TAKE MY EMBROIDERY WITH ME SO I HAVE something to do when I'm traveling or even waiting for an appointment, and a simple, uncomplicated design like this all-in-one sampler is easy to pick up or put down quickly. Just choose the size embroidery hoop you'd like to use and then select striking color combinations of solid fabric and perle cotton. No transferring, tracing, or formal pattern is needed— only a quick round of marking out the section lines and filling in everything just the way you like it!

I've stitched the same little five-part design in hoops from 3 in. to 8 in. in diameter (see p. 61). I love how the scale and colors of threads and fabrics change the feel while letting the ultra-simple design and your own hand-stitching shine. Make several of these in different sizes or color stories, and display them as a pretty collection on your wall.

WHAT YOU'LL NEED

- Embroidery Kit (pp. 8–10)
- Wooden embroidery hoop, between 3 in. and 8 in. diameter
- 1 piece of solid background fabric that measures 3 in. larger than the hoop size; I like to use quilting cotton weight
- 1 piece of muslin that measures 3 in. larger than the hoop size for the backing
- Perle cotton or floss, in one or several colors
- Water-soluble fabric marking pen (or tailor's chalk) in contrasting color to the fabric
- Quilting ruler
- Iron and distilled water in a spray bottle

techniques used
Preparing a hoop, *p. 18*
Marking fabric, *p. 19*
Embroidery, *pp. 20-24*

1. Press the two layers of fabric and prepare them so the surface fabric is smooth and taut in the embroidery hoop (see p. 18). Choose your perle cotton color or set of colors by holding the threads up to the fabric. You may want to make everything monochromatic, use a contrast color for the section lines, or use a harmonious mix of colors for the different stitches. Take a photo and see how the thread(s) and background fabric look together.

2. Mark section lines as shown in the diagram at right (**a**). Measuring or simply eyeballing, place a quilting ruler horizontally over the fabric in the hoop one-third of the way down from the top. Mark a straight line from side to side with the marking pen.

3. Use the ruler and pen to divide the top third in half vertically.

4. Below the horizontal line, mark off about a third of the open area, on the left side.

5. Finally, divide the open area to the right in half vertically and draw a line. You'll have five sections roughly the same size. Fill in with stitches however you like.

6. Backstitch all the section lines with perle cotton. I like to work from the top of the hoop to the bottom, but you can do these in any order.

7. If you don't want to embroider each section freehand, use a guideline for more even spacing. Mark horizontal stitch rows like you did in the embroidery sampler with a ruler aligned vertically at the center, marking small dots at even increments—I marked every ¼ in., working from top to bottom. Then, flip your ruler horizontally and trace straight lines from side to side at each marked dot. These will be your stitching guidelines.

8. Fill in each section with rows of different stitches. I chose to place my running stitches in the top left corner. If you marked stitching lines, you can simply follow them, or stitch more lines in between, more densely (as in my aqua sampler). If you're using the same color thread for stitching throughout, you can extend rows of running stitches from side to side in that whole top area and make your tiny crosses at the same time.

9. If you're using different colors, knot the perle cotton on the back of the first section of running stitches when you finish it. Thread the needle with a new strand of perle cotton and add rows of crosses to fill the upper right section the same way.

10. Fill in the lower left (tallest) section with cross-stitch Xs. I used the guideline as the midpoint of my Xs.

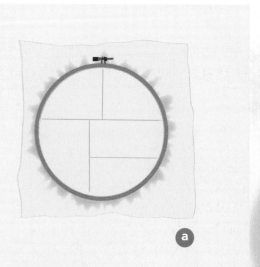

(a)

take it further

Design your own sampler to create a truly original work of art. Here are a few other ideas: Divide the fabric into 4, 6, or 8 symmetrical sections radiating out from the center like wedges of a pie, make an alphabet in backstitch with lazy daisies as flourishes, stitch a line of poetry or a meaningful saying, or mark and then stitch a child's artwork (see p. 63 for more ideas on this).

11. Now, add chain stitches to the middle right section, parallel to the Xs if you like the continuity.

12. To finish, fill in the final bottom right section with lazy daisies. I made mine about twice as big as simple lines of stitching, so about ½ in. (two lines) each.

13. When you're done stitching, take the sampler out of the hoop, carefully remove all fabric pen markings with distilled water, and press. Place the piece back in the hoop, positioning it so the stitched lines are neat and straight. Finish your piece for display. For directions on making the piping "framing" I added to the samplers shown here, go to sewplusquilt.com.

make it simpler

Make a smaller size sampler with a 3-in., 4-in., or 5-in. hoop and using all one color of floss. Stitching the little areas will go quickly, and you won't have to stop to change thread colors!

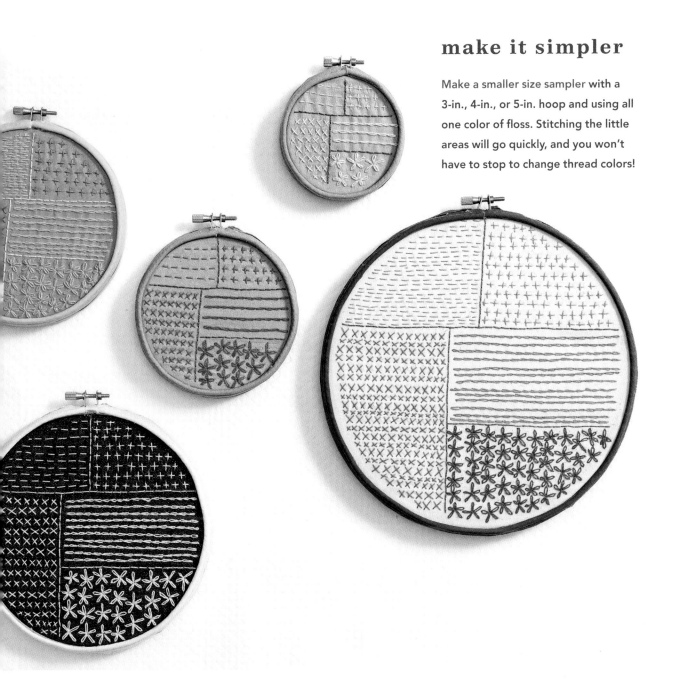

memento embroidery artwork

TRANSFORM A CHILD'S ARTWORK, A TREASURED LOVE
letter, a grandparent's handwriting, or any other
special memento by stitching it onto fabric
to keep forever. This is a very personal and
adaptable project and a beautiful way to spend a
bit of creative time. Use any stitches you like, or
keep it as simple as backstitching—the perfect
outline stitch for embellishing handwriting or
drawing with thread.

For my memento embroidery pieces, I asked
each of my kids to draw on muslin in a hoop
using a water-soluble fabric marker so I could
stitch over their artwork in different colors. Be
sure to have your artist sign and date the work,
and take a photo in case it fades or gets wet
before you have a chance to finish stitching.

Note: If you want to trace a special design or
handwritten message on paper instead of working from original drawings like these, I recommend using transfer paper or the method of your
choice for tracing and marking your fabric. Simply follow the package directions and then stitch
the lines or letters as you go.

WHAT YOU'LL NEED

- Embroidery Kit (pp. 8–10)
- Perle cotton or floss in colors of your choice
- 5-in. or 6-in. wooden embroidery hoop
- 2 pieces of muslin measuring 2 in. larger than the hoop
- Water-soluble fabric marking pen

1. Position the two layers of pressed muslin
in the embroidery hoop, tightening the hoop
so the fabric is neat and taut.

2. Using a fabric marker, write or draw your
original design directly onto the top layer of
muslin. Be sure to leave a ½-in. perimeter
around the hoop, which won't be stitched.
Take a photo of the drawing or design for
reference.

3. Using a backstitch (or any stitch of your
choice), follow the lines of the writing or
drawing with embroidery. Use as many or as
few colors as you like within the design.

4. To "frame" your stitching in the hoop like I
did, see sewplusquilt.com.

techniques used

Cutting, *pp. 25–26*
Preparing a hoop, *p. 18*
Marking fabric, *p. 19*
Embroidery, *pp. 20–24*

make it simpler

Use just one color of perle cotton or floss to complete the work, for a monochromatic approach.

take it further

Make a series of these pieces, having your child create one each year, then finish them as the center of a patchwork quilt block or wall piece. Or transfer and stitch a favorite family recipe or a special note in a loved one's handwriting, and share it with family or friends.

echo-quilted pillows

THIS IS A FUN PROJECT THAT EMBELLISHES AND ENHANCES a favorite bold print or your own hand-dyed fabrics, with hand-quilting as simple as the running stitches you mastered in your samplers. When you layer a focus fabric over batting and muslin backing and take the time to hand-quilt intuitive echo designs, the texture and charm bring a print or pattern to life. You can choose thread in a calm, coordinating color or a vivid contrast hue for more pop.

I originally hand-quilted some of my favorite graphic quilting cotton prints for my pillows, and then last summer, my friend Meredith invited me over to try indigo dyeing for the first time. I wrapped rubber bands and twine around sections of plain muslin, which created organic white circular shapes within the soft blue background. I got inspired to trace the shapes with radiating rows of contour stitching inside and out—the perfect portable summer stitching project!

WHAT YOU'LL NEED

- Embroidery Kit (pp. 8–10)
- Pillow form
- Printed quilting cotton or hand-dyed fabric for the pillow front and back, 1 in. larger than the pillow form
- Perle cotton or floss in colors of your choice
- Batting measuring 2 in. larger than the pillow form
- Muslin measuring 2 in. larger than the pillow form
- Invisible zipper, sized to fit your pillow (a few inches shorter is ideal)

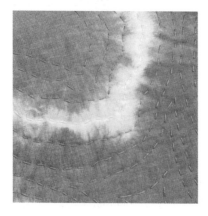

techniques used

Basting, *p. 46*
Quilting, *pp. 46–47*
Adding an invisible
zipper, *p. 30*
Edgestitching, *p. 27*
Clipping corners, *p. 29*

1. Make a quilt sandwich by pressing and layering the pillow front, batting, and muslin. Hand-baste the layers with big running stitches in a contrast color of regular sewing thread.

2. Starting from a central area of your design, use the perle cotton to hand-quilt around the lines of the design, leaving as much space between the design and stitching line as you like. I stitched just outside the designs of each of my printed cotton fabrics, both for texture and to draw the eye to the patterns.

3. Continue hand-stitching from the center area outward. Smooth the layers as you go so they don't bunch or wrinkle as you stitch; you won't need a hoop for this project unless you really want to keep things precise.

4. For a more organic look or to fill negative space, you can hand-quilt ripples or contour lines within, or outward from, a shape or pattern of the design.

make it simpler

Choose a very simple repeating design for your fabric print, and follow it closely, rather than improvising contour lines.

take it further

Make a beautiful whole cloth wall or baby quilt by using this same intuitive technique on a larger scale.

HERE'S MY ADVICE

Choose a print with a bold design or interesting shapes to inspire your embroidery. I used designs by Anna Maria Horner and Lotta Jansdotter. If you are hand-dyeing fabrics, leave some areas undyed using the methods of your choice to spark your hand-stitching ideas!

For my organic indigo circles, I stitched within the undyed rings with a soft off-white perle cotton, then stitched contoured curved lines outward, following the shape. This is a very personal, intuitive process; you can quilt your lines closely together or leave more negative space. As my rings began to grow outward and then meet, I stitched more curves and echoes to fill the rest of the square top.

5. When you are happy with your overall design, press it lightly, then pin and machine-stitch the perimeter of the square, ¼ in. from the edges of the focus fabric. Trim the excess batting and muslin and square up.

6. Add an invisible zipper to the bottom edge of the pillow's front and back panels, then stitch the perimeter with a ½-in. seam allowance, clip corners, and turn right side out (see pp. 29–30 for more information).

HERE'S MY ADVICE

Cutting your pillow front and back pieces 1 in. larger than the pillow itself will create a neat cover that fits smoothly over the pillow—sewing with the ½-in. seam allowance will leave you with a cover exactly the size of the pillow, so it fits smoothly over it. If you prefer a closer "stuffed" fit, or use a flatter pillow form without much loft, you can cut your fabrics to the exact measurement of the pillow form, sew a cover 1 in. smaller than the pillow, and tuck it inside.

sashiko drawstring bag

I LOVE SASHIKO—A TRADITIONAL JAPANESE FORM OF FOLK art embroidery where simple stitches can create a striking geometric pattern or add new life to a special piece. This handmade project bag keeps your embroidery supplies neatly tucked inside, thanks to a bright contrast drawstring. Adding your own sashiko-style embellishments makes it beautiful as well as useful.

WHAT YOU'LL NEED

- Embroidery Kit (pp. 8–10)
- Perle cotton or floss in colors of your choice; I used off-white, yellow, blue, and green
- 8-in. to 10-in. (or smaller) wooden embroidery hoop
- ½ yd. lightweight denim or other solid-colored fabric
- Muslin measuring 13 in. x 16 in.
- ½ yd. quilting cotton for the lining
- Tailor's chalk
- Rotary cutter, quilting ruler, and mat
- 25-mm binding tape maker
- Iron with spray bottle of distilled water
- Sewing machine with thread to match the denim and lining
- Straight pins

techniques used

Cutting, *pp. 25–26*
Embroidery, *pp. 20–24*
Sewing seams, *pp. 26–27*
Clipping corners, *p. 29*
Making binding, *p. 28*
Topstitching, *p. 27*

cutting key	Denim	Muslin	Lining
Outer bag	One 13-in. x 16-in. piece One 12-in. x 15-in. piece	One 13-in. x 16-in. piece	
Lining			Two 12-in. x 15-in. pieces
Drawstring and casing	One 4-in. x 29-in. piece		One 2-in. x WOF strip

MAKE THE BAG

1. Following the Cutting Key, cut the denim, muslin, and lining fabrics using a rotary cutter, quilt ruler, and cutting mat.

2. You'll begin by embroidering a design on the larger (13 in. x 16 in.) piece of denim for the sashiko side (front) of your bag. Position the denim over the muslin, right side facing up, and press the pieces together so they're neatly aligned. Working from the center of the denim, mark the stitching area with a 7-in.-long x 6-in.-wide rectangle (or the size of your choice) with chalk. I stitched my sashiko design freehand, but if you'd like, you can use chalk to mark horizontal guidelines every ½ in.

3. Place the denim and muslin in the embroidery hoop, and embroider rows of stitches in any colors of your choosing. I stitched rows of tiny crosses, running stitches, and Xs in a repeating pattern of colors. If you're using a smaller embroidery hoop, you may need to unscrew the clasp and reposition the fabric as you stitch.

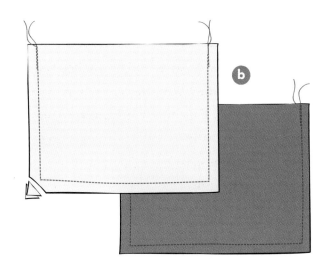

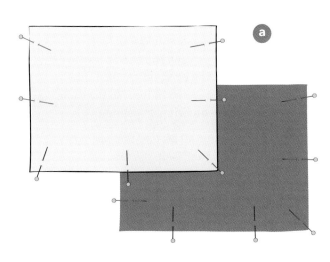

4. Press the finished stitched piece and trim it to 12 in. x 15 in. Pin and machine-stitch the perimeter of the two pieces of aligned fabrics, ¼ in. from the edge of the fabrics.

5. Press the second piece of denim outer bag fabric and both lining fabric pieces.

6. Pin the sashiko-stitched denim to the plain denim along three edges, right sides facing, leaving the top (15-in.) edge open (**a**).

7. Stitch the three sides of the outer bag together with a ½-in. seam allowance, backstitching at the beginning and end to secure the seam. Clip the bottom two corners (**b**).

8. Repeat steps 6 and 7 to pin, stitch, and clip the lining fabrics the same way.

9. Press the side seams of both the outer bag and the lining open. Press ½ in. down to the wrong side of both the denim and lining bag sections.

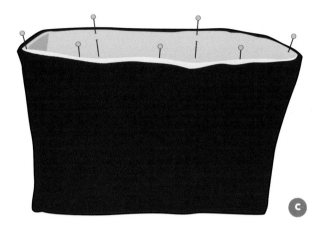

10. Turn the denim bag right side out, gently opening the corners with a pencil or chopstick, and tuck the lining inside it so that the wrong sides of the fabrics are facing. Pin around the opening, aligning the folded edges neatly, so all raw edges are tucked between the lining and bag (c). Edge-stitch around the perimeter of the opening to join the layers.

MAKE THE DRAWSTRING AND CASING

11. Now use the 2-in. x WOF strip of lining to make a drawstring and the 4-in. x 29-in. strip of denim to make a simple casing.

12. To create the drawstring, use the binding tape maker to fold and press the lining strip into a ½-in.-wide drawstring. Pin along the long open edge and edgestitch the length of it to secure, then pivot at the end of the strip to turn and stitch the short end. Pivot again to stitch the folded long edge.

13. To create the casing, fold and press ½ in. to the wrong side along each of the long edges of the denim strip. Then mark the center point of the short edge, fold, and press to neatly catch the raw edges inside the casing, as if you're creating an oversized binding tape (d). Finally, open the casing again and fold and press the two short edges ½ in. to the wrong side. Stitch the two folded short sides down securely with a straight stitch (e).

14. Now press the long, folded edge of the denim casing one more time, and pin. Edgestitch along the fold to create a crisp, neat top of the casing.

15. To attach the casing, first fold it in half, approximately 14 in. on each side, and press to mark the centerline. Align the centerline with one side seam of your joined bag and lining. Pin the casing in place, over the edgestitched bag opening.

16. Now pin the casing all around the perimeter of the bag opening, working from the first side seam to the other. Then pin the other half of the casing to the bag in the same way (f). Check to make sure the casing is straight and aligned neatly.

make it simpler

Use 40 in. of a sturdy ribbon or cord for the drawstring. You'll need ⅓ yd. of lining if you use ribbon, and skip steps 11 and 12.

take it further

Make a whole set of these bags and use one for each working project. Instead of the 12-in.-wide x 15-in.-long dimensions you used for this version, make a smaller bag (cutting outer and lining sections 9 in. wide x 11 in. long, with a 4-in. x 20-in. casing) or a larger one (cutting outer and lining sections 15 in. wide x 18 in. long, with a 4-in. x 34-in. casing). Leave the drawstring the same length, or adjust it longer if you like by sewing two 2-in. sections together.

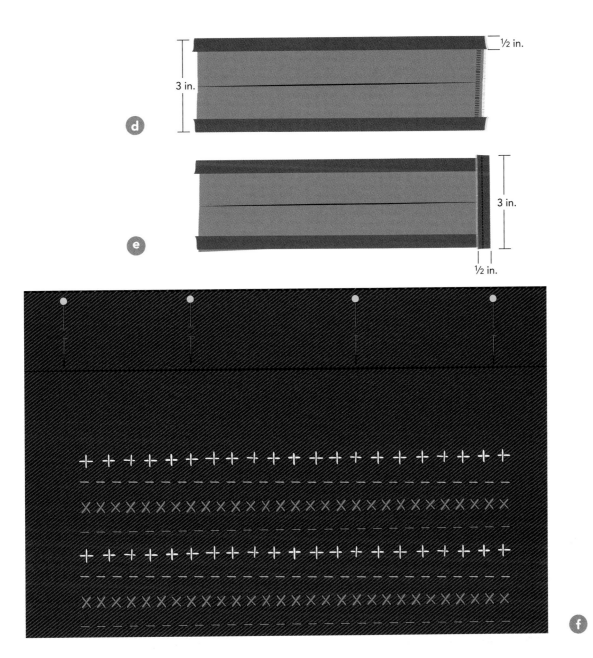

17. Edgestitch the casing, catching all layers of the bag inside the folds and backstitching at the beginning and end of the seam. Check to make sure the seamline doesn't waver and miss catching the fabrics on the other side, and resew any sections if need be.

18. Using a safety pin, guide the drawstring through the casing. Trim both ends of the drawstring with scissors or pinking shears, and tie a knot at each end. Trim all threads. Your bag is ready to use!

square within a square log cabin pillows

Finished size: 16 in. square
Seam allowance: ¼ in.

QUILT BLOCKS MAKE WONDERFUL PILLOW COVERS, BUT there's something charming about a log cabin design that "frames" a pretty print or color with a series of squares radiating outward—exactly how I made my very first patchwork project! I mixed vintage fabrics and Denyse Schmidt's Flea Market Fancy prints with reclaimed corduroy from an old pair of Levi's, and loved how the prints and contrast solid squares worked together.

I've made dozens of these fun pillows since then, and wanted to share a few of my favorites here, including the Golden Mustang, which uses scraps from the Golden Rays Quilt (p. 120). This is a perfect second patchwork project after the sampler— intuitive, simple, and a lot of fun!

WHAT YOU'LL NEED

- Sewing + Quilting Kit (pp. 10–13)
- 1 charm square (5 in.) of a favorite fabric for the center
- Two 1½-in. x WOF strips of a contrast color for the first and third tiers of logs (approximately 70 in. long)
- One 2-in. x WOF strip of a print for the second tier of logs (approximately 36 in. long)
- One and one-half 3-in. x WOF strips of a finishing print for the fourth tier of logs (approximately 56 in. long)
- Batting measuring 18 in. square
- Muslin measuring 18 in. square
- Perle cotton and hand-quilting needle

To finish with an envelope back, you'll need:

- 2 pieces of backing fabric measuring 16½ in. x 11 in. and 16½ in. x 9 in.
- 17-in. length of handmade or store-bought ½-in. double-fold binding tape

OR

To finish with an invisible zipper, you'll need:

- Backing fabric measuring 16½ in. square (I used the same gold pearl bracelets as the outermost square on the front)
- One 14-in. invisible zipper and invisible zipper foot

techniques used

Pressing, *pp. 24–25*
Cutting, *pp. 25–26*
Log cabin piecing, *pp. 32–35*
Machine-quilting, *p. 54*
Hand-quilting, *p. 55*
Invisible zipper, *p. 30*
Envelope back, *p. 29*

cutting key	A (assorted solids)	B (solid)	C (contrast print)	D (coordinating print)
Center square	One 5-in. square			
First and third tier of logs		Two 1½-in. x WOF strips (about 70 in. total)		
Second tier of logs			One 2-in. x WOF strip (about 36 in. in length)	
Borders				One and one-half 3-in. x WOF strips (about 56 in. total)
Invisible zipper finish back panel				One 16½-in. square
Envelope back finish back panel				One 16½-in. x 11-in. panel One 16½-in. x 9-in. panel 17-in. strip of double-fold binding

CUTTING + PIECING

1. Cut and press all fabrics you'll use to construct your block (see the Cutting Key). Using the basic log cabin piecing technique (pp. 32–35) and working clockwise, add a first tier of logs to your center square with a 1½-in. strip in a contrast color. Press seams outward and square up the block.

2. Continue building the block the same way, using the 2-in. strip for the second tier and the same 1½-in. strip for the third tier, pressing and squaring up when you complete each tier.

3. Finish the log cabin block by adding the 3-in. strip to make a block 16½ in. square. Press and square up.

ASSEMBLE THE PILLOW COVER

4. Make a quilt sandwich. Lay the muslin face down, position the batting on top, and center the quilt block face up over the batting, making sure all layers are smooth and aligned.

5. Hand-baste the layers together (or use the basting method of your choice).

6. Starting with the first square of logs around the center square, use machine-quilting to outline ⅛ in. around the square, catching the seams underneath, turning corners at a 90-degree angle, and backstitching at the end to hold the quilting line securely. Change thread colors to coordinate with your fabrics if you like, or just use a neutral color for consistency.

7. Repeat to outline-quilt the other three squares the same way.

8. Hand-quilt just outside each of the machine-quilting outline squares with a running stitch in a contrasting perle cotton.

9. Lightly press the pillow front, machine-stitch around the perimeter, and trim excess batting and muslin to leave the block at 16½ in. square.

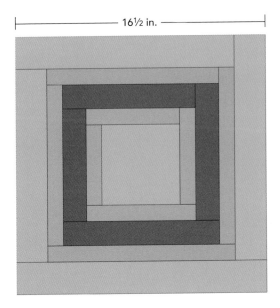

⊢————— 16½ in. —————⊣

TO FINISH WITH
AN INVISIBLE ZIPPER

10. Following the directions for inserting an invisible zipper (p. 30), measure, mark, and match the zipper with the bottom edge of the pillow front and stitch in place. Repeat with the backing fabric. Stitch the perimeter of the pillow cover, clip corners, and turn right side out.

TO FINISH WITH
AN ENVELOPE BACK

11. Press the backing panels. Pin binding tape to the 16½-in. (long) edge of the 11-in. panel, right sides together; stitch the binding down securely. Fold and press ½ in. to the wrong side of the 9-in. backing panel, then fold and press again. Sew this double-fold section to finish the edge (this side will not be seen from the back of the pillow).

12. Place the pillow front on a work surface, right side up. Layer the 11-in.-wide back panel with the binding edge over it, with right sides facing and matching corners and edges on the sides, top, and bottom. Pin in place.

13. Now place the smaller panel right side down over the other two layers. Align it with the left edge of the pillow front so it's overlapping the binding edge by several inches. Pin around the perimeter, making sure the overlapped area is securely pinned, neat, and flat.

14. Stitch the perimeter of the panels using a ¼-in. seam allowance; clip corners and turn right side out. Slip a pillow form through the envelope closure.

make it simpler

Use just two fabrics to radiate outward from the center square instead of a variety. Choosing two print fabrics from the same designer's collection or using a pair of solids that complement each other nicely makes a very harmonious design. Even faster, use jelly roll (2½-in. x WOF) strips all around a charm square instead of cutting various-width strips one by one. Of course, this will alter the size of your finished pillow.

take it further

To make a striking 12-in. x 16-in. rectangular pillow, follow the same basic instructions for the original outline- and hand-quilted mustang version, but cut your fabrics this way:

• One 8-in. x 4-in. center rectangle plus two 2½-in. x WOF strips from your main fabric (I used Anna Maria Horner's roses on gold; leftovers from the second strip became the 12½-in. binding tape for the envelope back).

• Two 1½-in. x WOF strips and two 10-in. x 12½-in. pieces of contrast fabric for the envelope back (I used Heather Ross's honey bees).

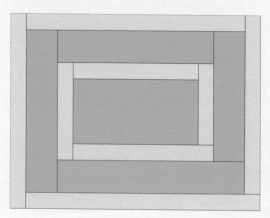

For a more balanced design, try a smaller center square with four additional squares radiating outward in the same width. This will give you the chance to use more scraps or prints. I've offered two different ways to remix the basic idea, so go with the style that appeals to you most, or put your own spin on it!

Note: I quilted both these pillow covers with a series of concentric squares spaced ½ in. apart in a neutral thread color.

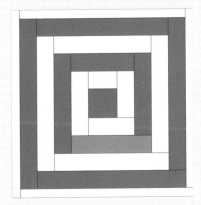

For the red and gold version you'll need:

- Color family 1 (I used red)
  - One 3-in. center square
  - One 2-in. x WOF strip for tier 2 logs
  - Two 3-in. x WOF strips for tier 4 logs
- Color family 2 (I used gold)
  - One 2-in. x WOF strip for tier 1 logs
  - Two 2-in. x WOF strips for tier 3 logs (use the leftovers of these strips to make the 17 in. of binding mentioned below)
  - One 16½-in. square for the backing and 14-in. invisible zipper

  OR

- 17-in. length of ½-in. double-fold binding and two pieces of backing fabric measuring 16½ in. x 11 in. and 16½ in. x 9 in. for envelope closure

1. Build the log cabin block the same way as the blue scrappy version, but alternate colors for the center square and tier 2 and 4 logs with tier 1 and 3 logs. The wider (3 in.) tier 4 logs will frame the block.

For both versions, follow the instructions for outline- and hand-quilting the front panel, adding an envelope back or an invisible zipper to finish your pillow.

For the blue scrappy version, you'll need:

- One 3-in. center square in a print of your choice
- 4 assorted prints, cut into 2-in. x 24-in. strips
- One contrast solid (I used white), two 2-in. x WOF strips (about 60 in. total) plus two 1-in. x WOF strips (about 64 in. total) for the outermost framing
- Batting measuring 18 in. square
- Muslin measuring 18 in. square
- One 16½-in. square for the backing and invisible zipper

  OR

- 17-in. length of ½-in. double-fold binding tape and two pieces of backing fabric measuring 16½ in. x 11 in. and 16½ in. x 9 in. for envelope pillow

1. Press all fabrics and add a first tier of logs (1–4) in contrast color B around the center square, pressing and trimming. Now add logs 5–8, using a different color A print for each one, pressing and trimming. Add logs 9–12 in the color B solid and logs 13–16 in color A prints. In this round, I chose to use each of my prints directly across the design from their first appearance for balance and variety. Finish the pillow cover block with a last tier of logs using the 1-in. strip of color B solid, then press and square up your block.

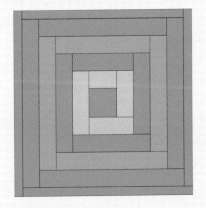

half-square triangle pinwheel pincushion

Finished size: 4 in. square
Seam allowance: ¼ in.

EVERY SEWIST AND QUILTER CAN USE A PINCUSHION, AND if you are planning to take your embroidery, hand-quilting, or sewing projects on a trip or to a sew day, a needle book is essential, too.

I designed a cheerful pinwheel pincushion and matching needle book with felt "pages" using bright prints from my friend Monica Solorio-Snow's charming Sew Yummy collection. I love how the prints brought the simple designs to life. You can use calm solids, colorful vintage prints, streamlined modern fabrics, or anything you like, but keep the scale of any print small enough to shine in these mini-blocks.

For a few other design ideas, see the sidebar on p. 82.

WHAT YOU'LL NEED

- Sewing + Quilting Kit (pp. 10–13), including invisible or matching thread

- Eight 3-in. squares of different coordinating prints, four in a dark-color and four in a light-color family (you can use two different prints for both the top and bottom, or four for more variation)

- A handful of polyfil stuffing

- 2 shank-style buttons (with a loop behind the button instead of holes for stitching it down)

techniques used

Pressing, *pp. 24–25*
Cutting, *pp. 25–26*
2-at-a-time
HST method, *p. 42*
Row assembly, *p. 50*
Clipping corners, *p. 29*
Edgestitching, *p. 27*
Hand-stitching, *pp. 20–24*

cutting key	A (dark prints)	B (light prints)
HST blocks	Four 3-in. squares (can be all the same or 2 each of 2 different prints)	Four 3-in. squares (can be all the same or 2 each of 2 different prints)

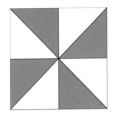 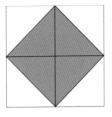

CUTTING + PIECING

1. Cut and press all fabrics you'll use to construct the blocks (see the Cutting Key).

2. Make four sets of 2-at-a-time HSTs from the squares. If you're using four prints, pair the same fabrics twice each to make two sets of 4 identical HSTs; if you're using two, you'll make 8 identical HSTs. Press and trim the 8 HST blocks to 2⅓ in. square.

 ### HERE'S MY ADVICE

With squares this small, I found that making the 2-at-a-time HST blocks was easier to handle than the 4-at-a-time method, which leaves bias edges vulnerable to stretching.

3. Divide the HST blocks into two sets of four, one for the front/top of the pincushion and one for the back/bottom. Choose a block layout for the HSTs—I used a pinwheel for the top and a diamond for the bottom.

4. Join each set, pinning and matching seams and pressing seams to one side. Nest seams when you join two sets together, then press that center seam open to reduce bulk.

ASSEMBLE THE PINCUSHION

5. Leaving a 1-in. opening at one side, pin the top and bottom blocks together, right sides facing and aligning edges and corners. Stitch with a ¼-in. seam allowance, backstitching at the beginning and end to hold the seam.

6. Clip corners, then turn the pincushion right side out, gently opening the corners with a pencil or bamboo skewer.

7. Stuff the pincushion with batting so it's nicely filled, then tuck the seams in and hand-stitch the opening closed with invisible or matching thread.

8. Stitch a button over the center of the top—the heart of the pinwheel in my design. Catch all layers with a few stitches, pulling them tight to tuft the pincushion.

19. Now add a second button on the bottom of the pincushion, stitching it securely. You can gently tilt your pincushion, almost folding it, to ease the needle through from one side to another and pass it through the shank of the button.

10. Securely knot the thread and hide it under one of the buttons.

pretty little rail fence
needle book

Finished size: 7 in. wide by 3½ in. high; 3½ in. square when closed
Seam allowance: ¼ in.

FOR MY NEEDLE BOOK, I PIECED TWO SIMPLE RAIL FENCE blocks and used them as the covers of my book, embroidering around one of the adorable motifs in Monica's print—a tomato pincushion! Sewing in a durable coordinating lining and four felt "pages" offers lots of places to store my pins, needles, safety pins, and needle threaders. A simple button-and-loop closure keeps everything secure and neat.

WHAT YOU'LL NEED

- Sewing + Quilting Kit (pp. 10–13)
- Scraps of 2 or 3 coordinating fabrics, A and B for the cover and C for the lining (you can also reuse one of the cover prints for this):
  - A: One 2-in. x 8-in. strip
  - B: Two 1½-in. by 8-in. strips
  - C: One 4-in. by 7½-in. rectangle
- Batting scrap measuring 4½ in. by 8 in.
- Remnant of wool felt for the "pages" measuring 3½ in. x 6 in.
- 1 small button
- 1 hair elastic

techniques used

Pressing, *pp. 24–25*
Cutting, *pp. 25–26*
Rail fence piecing, *pp. 38–39*
Machine-quilting, *p. 54*
Embroidery, *pp. 20–24*
Edgestitching , *p. 27*
Hand-stitching, *pp. 20–24*
Clipping corners, *p. 29*

cutting key	A (print)	B (contrast print)	C (solid or repeat of one of an A or B fabric)	Wool felt
Rail fence blocks	2-in. x 8-in. strip	Two 1½-in. x 8-in. strips		
Lining			4-in. x 7½-in. rectangle	
Pages				Two 3½-in. x 6-in. rectangles

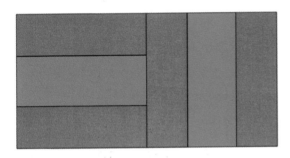

CUTTING + PIECING

1. Press and cut all fabrics you'll use to construct the needle book (see the Cutting Key).

2. Position, pin, and sew the three 8-in.-long strips together into a simple rail fence block with a strip of A centered between two strips of B. Press the seams away from the center. Using a rotary cutter and quilt ruler, cut the pieced strip in half and trim to make two 4-in. squares. These will be the front and back covers of your book.

ASSEMBLE THE NEEDLE BOOK

3. Choose the position of the block for the front and back. I used a vertical setting for the front and a horizontal one for the back. Align the squares, right sides facing, and machine-stitch to join them, again using a ¼-in. seam allowance. This seam will be the "spine" of the book. The cover should now measure 4 in. wide and 7½ in. long.

4. Layer the cover right side up over the scrap of batting and pin or baste it in place. Stitch along the rail fence block seams to join them to the batting, either using a straight stitch to quilt them as stitch-in-the-ditch or a narrow zigzag as a decorative element (which is what I chose to do).

5. Press the cover, machine-stitch around the perimeter, and square it up, trimming excess batting.

6. If you'd like to embellish your cover with any embroidery, stitch the design of your choice now. I outlined the tiny tomato pincushions with backstitch in matching perle cotton.

7. Press your embellished cover. Pin it to the lining piece with right sides facing, aligning edges and corners and leaving a 2-in. opening at the center of the back cover (**a**); see p. 82. Stitch the layers together all the way around the perimeter, leaving the opening and backstitching at the beginning and end to hold the seam. Clip the corners and turn right side out, gently opening the corners with a pencil or bamboo skewer. Press the cover and lining so it lies smooth and flat.

8. Cut a 1½-in. length of a hair elastic and make a loop, holding the cut ends together. Fold in and press the raw edges of the opening ¼ in., slip the cut ends of the hair elastic inside, and pin securely, so a loop measuring about 1 in. extends out of the pinned cover (**b**). Edgestitch the entire perimeter of the "book," catching the elastic loop within the seam, and backstitch to secure the beginning and end.

9. Layer the two pieces of felt together (trim with pinking shears for a decorative edge, if you like), center over the lining of your book, and pin in place. Stitch a straight seam up the center to bind the pages into the book, backstitching at the beginning and end of the seam (**c**).

10. Using the loop to guide your placement, hand-sew a small button on the front cover (**d**). Now add pins, needles, and safety pins to the pages and inside covers, and use a larger safety pin to corral needle threaders or other handy notions.

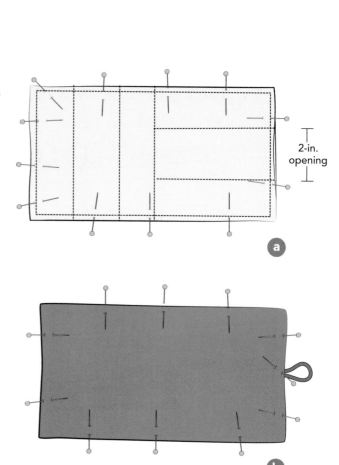

2-in. opening

make it simpler

Make both projects with a single fabric instead of patchwork. Just cut two 4-in. squares for the pincushion and a 7 ½-in. by 4-in. piece for the needle book cover (the same as the lining), and skip the steps for piecing the blocks.

take it further

Add a pocket on the inside of the needle book by hand or machine, using wool felt. Or add more embroidery to either project; if it's a gift, consider including the recipient's name or favorite motif.

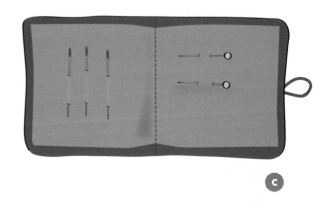

radiating diamonds string tote bag

Finished size: 15½-in. x 15½-in. bag with 28-in. straps
Seam allowances: ¼ in. (patchwork piecing) and ½ in. (bag)

THIS STRIKING TOTE BAG USES STRING BLOCKS IN TWO settings to form a vivid diamond on one side and Roman stripe diagonals on the other. Using precut roll-up strips (I chose 2½-in. strips of beautiful monochromatic prints from Carolyn Friedlander) for the patchwork makes it quick to sew, and using denim for the foundation "muslin" keeps it sturdy and durable. Handmade covered buttons that match one of the prints add a beautifully personalized touch.

WHAT YOU'LL NEED

- Sewing + Quilting Kit (pp. 10–13)

- 12 or more precut roll-up strips (2½ in. x WOF) from one fabric collection, in one color family. If you want to piece a symmetrical diamond design like mine, it's most successful if you have three strips of one focus fabric (for example, the crosshatch I used as the background as the center diagonal and at both corners) that frame the other prints so they pop. The other nine roll-up strips can be assorted or also repeat. For more variety, use a larger number of strips with fewer repeats.

- ½ yd. of light- or medium-weight denim

- ½ yd. of lining fabric

- 60 in. of webbing for the tote straps

- ¾-in. and 1⅞ -in. covered button kits (one each)

- 1 hair elastic

techniques used

Pressing, *pp. 24–25*
Cutting, *pp. 25–26*
String blocks piecing,
pp. 40–41
Row assembly, *p. 50*
Seams, *pp. 26–27*

cutting key	A (assorted prints)	B (denim/medium-weight fabric)	C (print contrast fabric)
String blocks	12 or more 2½-in. x WOF strips, including 3 of one fabric to use as the background if you want to create a contrast diamond design		
Foundation squares		Eight 8½-in. squares	
Lining			Two 16½-in. squares

CUTTING + PIECING

1. Press the fabrics (use Best Press on the denim) and cut them according to the Cutting Key. Trim selvages and arrange the duplicate focus fabric strips together.

2. If you want to make a symmetrical diamond design, you'll piece those four blocks first and make each of them identical. In my layout, I'll call my background fabric (the crosshatch in the center and corners) A, light gray contrast B, and darker gray contrast C—the diamond that pops in the final design. Start block 1 with a strip of A as the center; position a strip of B over it and stitch down the right edge with a ¼-in. seam allowance. Trim. Repeat, adding A and B strips together to start forming blocks 2, 3, and 4. Press them well.

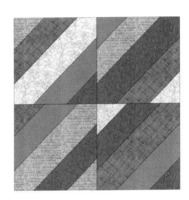

3. Now sew a strip of C to the opposite edge of the A strip for blocks 1–4 and trim, then press. Arrange the blocks together so strip C forms a diamond, tucking any extra fabric under and out of the way, and make sure the diagonal lines align nicely and the piecing is accurate. Gently seam-rip and adjust if necessary.

4. Now add strips of A to both the B and C sides of each block, building outward toward the corners. If your fabric strips don't quite reach the corner, you can piece in a smaller scrap or angled cut piece to bridge the gap. Press.

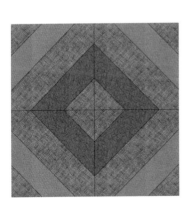

5. Using an 8½-in. square template or a quilt ruler and rotary cutter, trim and square up the diamond string blocks. Save all your scraps.

ASSEMBLE THE TOTE

6. Arrange blocks 1, 2, 3, and 4 into a diamond layout and begin assembling the front of your tote bag by pinning blocks 1 + 2 together to create the top half of the diamond. Pin where the angles meet to get an exact color match. Sew with a ¼-in. seam allowance.

7. Pin and stitch blocks 3 + 4 the same way. Press the blocks 1 + 2 row seam to the left and the blocks 3 + 4 row seam to the right. Now pin the two rows together, nesting seams and pinning where angles meet for an exact color match. Sew with a ¼-in. seam allowance. Press, stitch the perimeter of the four-block unit to catch any bias seams, and set aside.

8. To make the Roman stripe blocks for the back of the tote bag, piece the other 4 string blocks with strips randomly placed; for example, I used 4 different prints for my center strips, varied where I placed other fabrics, and intentionally tried not to match any of them. Piece and press your blocks until they are complete, then trim them to 8⅜ in. square.

9. Decide on the layout, orienting each block in the same direction, and join blocks 5 + 6 and 7 + 8, followed by the two rows, nesting seams as you did in steps 6 and 7. Press and stitch around the perimeter.

10. Pin the two bag panels with right sides together around three sides, matching corners and edges, and leaving the top open. Stitch with a ½-in. seam allowance, backstitching at the beginning and end to hold the seam. Clip the corners.

11. Cut two 16½-in. squares of lining fabric and pin them together around three sides, right sides facing, but leave a 6-in. opening at the bottom. Sew the lining panels together with a ½-in. seam allowance, backstitching at the beginning and end to hold the seam, and leaving the opening unsewn. Clip the corners (**a**).

12. Turn the lining right side out and slip it into the bag with right sides facing and matching side seams. Measure 3 in. in from each side seam on the front and back, and mark each of those spots with a pin.

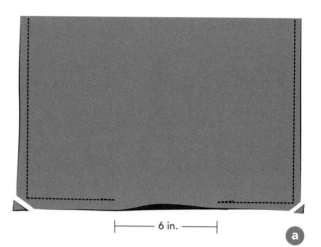

|— 6 in. —| **a**

13. Cut the strip of webbing into two 30-in. straps. Being careful not to twist it, slide one strap between the front of the tote and the lining. Pin one raw edge securely at each marked spot, making sure at least ¼ in. of webbing extends up above the fabric edges (**b**).

14. Repeat step 13 to slip the second strap between the back of the tote bag and the lining, pinning in place.

15. Cut a 2½-in. to 3-in. piece of the hair elastic and form a loop, holding the raw edges together. Mark the center of the back at the seam between blocks 5 and 6, and tuck the elastic loop in between the

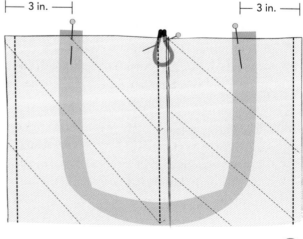

|— 3 in. —| |— 3 in. —|

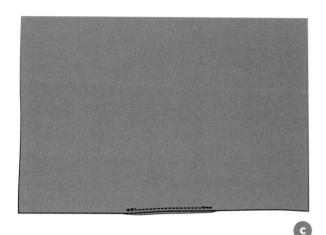

(c)

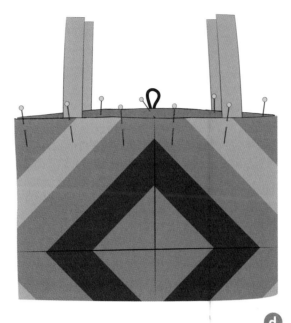

(d)

back and lining. Pin it securely, with raw edges extending up the same way as the webbing (b).

16. Pin the rest of the way around the top of the bag, making sure seams and straps match and the loop is securely in place.

17. Stitch the perimeter of the tote's opening using a ½-in. seam allowance, and stitch over the strap areas a second time to reinforce them.

18. Gently turn the entire bag right side out through the opening in the lining. If either of the handles is crooked or if the loop is off, turn it back to wrong side out, gently rip out the seam, and move the handle to the correct spot; then repin and resew.

19. Once you are happy with the bag straps' place-ment and appearance, hand- or machine-stitch the opening in the lining closed (c).

20. Press all around the perimeter of the bag's opening, so the lining and outer bag are smooth and aligned. Pin the layers together and edgestitch the perimeter (d).

21. Following the package directions, make covered buttons in both sizes (I used my B fabric; you can piece smaller sections together from scraps if need be). Stitch the larger button in the center of the diamond and the smaller one at the top center of the front so the loop provides a secure closure.

make it simpler

Piece all the string blocks randomly instead of matching angles in identical blocks. Use any setting you like—diamond, X, Roman stripes, or chevron.

take it further

Make your own matching bag straps instead of using store-bought webbing.

Cut two 2½-in. by 30-in. strips of roll-up fabric, then use a double-fold technique like the casing for the drawstring bag (pp. 70–71) to fold and press raw edges inside. Edgestitch both long ends of each handle, and insert in the bag following the instructions here.

87

PART TWO

quilts

Now that you've had a chance to piece each of the four quilt blocks—log cabin, rail fence, string, and half-square triangle—and have gotten a bit of practice using them in smaller projects, you can make any (or all!) of the quilts in this book.

Whether you have a new baby to welcome in your friends' circle, a wedding or an anniversary coming up, a housewarming to celebrate, or just want to make something pretty and fun for yourself, here's a whole collection of beginner-friendly quilts. I've also added ways to simplify the designs or take them one step further, as well as tips, alternative settings, ways to change color or scale, and lots more options to make them your own.

Everyday Quilts p. 90
Let's start with some everyday favorite quilts, perfect for a cozy evening at home, bringing along on a picnic, or displaying on your wall.

Baby Quilts p. 103
Baby quilts are so much fun to make, especially if you keep them simple and machine washable—save the heirloom lace and embroidery for another project! Put your own spin on either of these

designs, or create a mini version to decorate the walls of a nursery.

Memento Quilts p. 112

Every quilt tells a story, but drawing on your own memories and experiences as inspiration can add deeper layers of beauty and meaning to even the simplest design. Whether you give a memento quilt as a gift or cherish it yourself, using special colors and fabrics creates a modern heirloom to treasure.

Kids' Quilts p. 120

A growing-up quilt for a child in your life should draw on all the joy, color, and personality he or she inspires. And making it in a generous size, as well as a fresh, fun style, will add years to its usefulness, from elementary school to a college dorm room!

Wedding + Anniversary Quilts p. 132

Traditionally, married couples started their new household with a hope chest of handmade linens and quilts, often contributed by friends and family. Times have changed quite a bit, but a handmade quilt is still a beautiful celebration of a new life together.

Celebration Quilts p. 144

Whether a gift for your sister's birthday, for a dear friend who is moving into a new home, or for any other occasion to celebrate, these quilts are joyful, beautiful, and easy to make.

floating crosses quilt

Finished block size: 7½ in. square
Finished size: 52 in. by 68 in.
Longarm quilted by Nancy Stovall with starbursts and diamonds
Seam allowance: ¼ in.

I LOVE PIECING STRING BLOCKS, AND I USUALLY MIX several colors within a single block—either carefully placed for an overall pattern of diamonds or chevrons, or randomly, for a bright, fun mix. I was so excited to work with my friend Elizabeth Hartman's Terrarium fabric collection, but once I saw the saturated, beautiful tones of her prints, I knew they would shine in monochromatic blocks. So five or six layouts on Quilt Canvas later, I came up with a design I really love.

The colorful, symmetrical patchwork crosses float over a calm background for lots of movement and color, with some of them partially disappearing at the edges. I've never made a quilt quite like it, and I love the effect! It's also a perfect size for cuddling when you're reading a book or watching a movie.

Using precut roll-up strips (jelly rolls) keeps the piecing fast. As an added bonus, you piece only 27 string blocks total, so this quilt comes together very quickly!

WHAT YOU'LL NEED

- Sewing + Quilting Kit, including an 8-in. quilting ruler (pp. 10–13)
- One jelly roll of a favorite fabric collection, or approximately forty 2½-in. x WOF strips that include duplicates or multiple options in three color families; I used Terrarium by Robert Kaufman Fabrics in the warm colorway (greens, browns, and oranges)
- 1⅜ yd. of 40-in.-wide muslin for foundation piecing
- 2 yd. of a solid or low-volume print for the background; I used Starburst by Robert Kaufman Fabrics in Ice Peach
- Batting measuring 56 in. x 72 in.
- Backing measuring 56 in. x 72 in.
- ½ yd. of fabric for binding, or 250 in./7 yd. of ½-in. double-fold binding tape; I used Starburst in Ice Peach

techniques used

Pressing, *pp. 24–25*

Cutting, *pp. 25–26*

Trimming, *p. 35*

Off-center string piecing, *pp. 40–41*

Quilt assembly, *p. 50*

Nesting seams, *p. 51*

Binding, *pp. 47–49*

If you're quilting this project at home, you'll also baste, mark, and quilt, *pp. 53–55*

cutting key	Muslin for foundation piecing	A/B/C (three color families' roll-up strips)	D (background fabric)
String blocks	Twenty-seven 8-in. squares	Forty 2½-in. x WOF strips, approximately 13-15 of each color family	
Background			Thirty-six 8-in. squares
Backing			56 in. x 72 in.
Binding			250 in. total of 2-in.-wide strips (thirteen 2-in. x WOF strips)

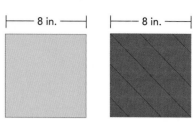

CUTTING + PIECING

1. Cut and press the fabrics following the Cutting Key on p. 91. It is easiest to cut the muslin and background fabric squares if you first cut 8-in. x WOF sections, then cut those into 8-in. squares.

2. Arrange the 2½-in. fabric strips into color families. I used green (A), brown (B), and orange (C).

3. Following the basic string-piecing instructions on p. 40 and using the alternative off-center diagonal placement, make 10 blocks in color A, 9 in color B, and 8 in color C, saving scraps as you piece to fill in corners. Press, trim, and set aside.

4. Following the diagram, lay out the quilt blocks and background squares in a 9 x 7-block grid to form the crosses pattern.

ASSEMBLE THE QUILT TOP

5. Label, stack, and assemble the rows. Press seams to one side when rows are assembled—odd rows (1, 3, 5, 7) to the left and even rows (2, 4, 6) to the right.

6. Join rows 1 + 2, 3 + 4, and 5 + 6 + 7. Then join sections 1 + 2 to 3 + 4, and finally join sections 1–4 to 5–7. Press all seams away from the center.

FINISH THE QUILT

7. You can hand- or machine-quilt, tie, or finish your quilt any way you like. I collaborated with my friend and longarm quilter Nancy Stovall to find stars and diamonds that beautifully complement Elizabeth's starburst fabric prints. If you are quilting your quilt, mark quilting lines with chalk, a fabric pen, or painter's tape.

8. Layer the quilt top, batting, and backing, then baste. Quilt or tie as desired, following your marked lines or tape.

9. After quilting or tying is complete, stitch the perimeter, trim excess batting and backing, and machine-bind (pp. 46–49).

make it simpler

For a super-fast version of this quilt (maybe your best friend's birthday is this weekend?), simply use three different colorful fabrics to cut as squares instead of piecing blocks for this design. You'll need ½ yd. each of fabrics A, B, and C; cut the number of 8-in. squares of each specified as pieced string blocks in the instructions, then assemble the same way using the same thirty-six 8-in. squares of fabric D as background.

take it further

Add more color throughout by making each of the six crosses (whole and partial) in a different monochromatic mix. You'll need strips of six different colors to make four sets of 5 blocks, one set of 4 blocks, and one set of 3 blocks. Keep the background as neutral as a single solid or as vibrant as you like.

basketweave picnic quilt

Finished block size: 6 in. square
Finished size: 64 in. x 50 in.
Machine-tied
Seam allowance: ½ in.

I WAS SO LUCKY TO TAKE A CLASS WITH FOUR OF THE quilters of Gee's Bend Quilters Collective at QuiltCon a few years ago. Their beautifully utilitarian quilts, which I'd seen in museums and at the Sisters Outdoor Quilt Show, inspired me to think about how to transform everyday garment fabrics into bold and engaging patchwork.

I chose a super-simple rail fence design in a basketweave setting, alternating vertical and horizontal blocks to draw the eye across the quilt, while keeping the placement of light, medium, and dark tones random within each block. Topstitching each seam in the quilt adds cohesiveness and a decorative element. I added a water-resistant, wipe-clean backing, so it's perfect for taking on an adventure or just out to the backyard.

WHAT YOU'LL NEED

- Sewing + Quilting Kit (pp. 10–13)
- 1 yd. each of three different shades of light- or medium-weight denim, 60 in. wide; I used Robert Kaufman light, medium, and dark indigo denim in 6½-oz. weight
- 68-in. x 54-in. lightweight batting; I recommend polyester batting, like Quilters Dream Green, instead of cotton for an outdoors picnic quilt
- 1½ yd. of 54-in.-wide wipe-clean laminated cotton for binding; I used a charming cat print from Robert Kaufman
- 7 yd. of flexible 1½-in.-wide poly-propylene webbing (recommended instead of cotton) for binding

techniques used

Cutting, *pp. 25-26*
Rail fence piecing, *pp. 38-39*
Topstitching, *p. 27*
Trimming, *p. 35*
Quilt assembly, *p. 50*
Basting, *p. 53*
Machine-tying, *p. 55*
Binding, *pp. 47-49*

cutting key	A (light denim)	B (medium denim)	C (dark denim)	Laminated cotton
Rail fence blocks	Ten 3-in. x 60-in. strips	Ten 3-in. x 60-in. strips	Ten 3-in. x 60-in. strips	
Backing				68 in. x 52 in.

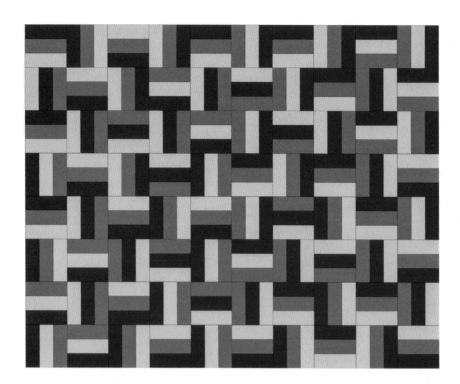

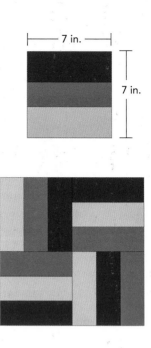

CUTTING

1. Cut all three denims with a rotary cutter and quilting ruler so you have ten 3-in. x WOF (60-in.) strips of each color (A, B, and C).

2. Remove any threads from the long strips of denim. Use light spray starch and an iron on the cotton setting to press each strip so it's smooth and the edges are crisp. Arrange the strips into stacks by color.

PLANNING + PIECING

3. You have two options for this project: make 80 identical blocks or mix up the color order for a variety of light and dark placement throughout. Since you can rotate and adjust blocks in the design, the real difference will be which color you use in the middle of the block. For example, blocks with strips in CAB order will look exactly the same as blocks with strips in BAC order if you flip one. I chose to alternate mine as much as possible for variety, so I made three sections each of ACB and CAB, and four of ABC (so 40 blocks have the

medium blue color in the middle, with 30 each of the others), which was perfect for a completely improvisational layout rather than a pattern. If you prefer a more orderly stairstep design repeating across the entire quilt, see Make It Simpler (facing page) for how to piece and lay out all 80 of your blocks with the same color order and orientation.

4. Make the first block section: Pick up one strip of each color (A, B, and C), and align A and B together all along one long edge. Pin (easiest for beginners) or simply hold them together, then stitch from selvage to selvage, using a ½-in. seam allowance, to create a 5-in. x 60-in. pieced section. Remember, you'll use a ½-in. seam allowance throughout.

5. Now align strip C over strip AB, with right sides facing, matching ends and edges, and join them with a ½-in. seam allowance. You'll now have three joined strips, in ABC order, measuring 7 in. x 60 in.

6. Press the back of the long joined strip sections, pressing all seams to the same side (it doesn't matter which way, but be consistent). Press the front the same way.

7. Now, topstitch each seam, catching all layers of the seam allowances in the topstitching. You can either pin all along the seam, or if you've pressed with light spray starch, you can simply stitch without pinning. I used a denim thread that worked well with all three colors.

8. Topstitch both long seams the entire width of the strips, ⅛ in. from the seam line. This is a long way to sew a single seam, but surprisingly fun! Set this section aside.

9. Now make nine more joined strip sections, using the three different denims in each one and topstitching each seam the same way.

make it simpler

Piece each block using the same color order, saving time on both piecing and following a planned instead of improvisational layout. When you lay out the blocks in the horizontal/vertical basketweave, you will see a striking color pattern emerge, almost like lightning streaks.

take it further

Make this an indoor quilt by piecing the top the same way but using batting of your choice and cotton backing measuring 54 in. x 68 in. Machine- or hand-tie all layers at the center of each block. Bind with 252 in./7 yd. of double-fold ½-in. cotton binding.

10. Once you have pieced, pressed, and topstitched all 10 sections, trim them into blocks. If you've pieced different color orders as I did, divide them into those groups and work with them one at a time. I started with my ABC blocks. Working from one end to the other of a joined ABC strip, use a rotary cutter and quilting ruler to trim the selvage edges on one side. Now cut the 60-in. section into 8 blocks, each measuring 7 in. square. They will appear identical to one another, with the middle strip narrower than the other two.

11. Cut the remaining ABC sections into 7-in.-square blocks the same way, then neatly stack all of them (in my case, 32 blocks from four sections) and put them in a labeled zip-top bag.

12. Now cut the other color order blocks by group—I cut 24 blocks from three strips of ACB and 24 blocks of three strips of BAC—and place them in separate bags, too. You will have a total of eighty 7-in.-square blocks. Square up any that are slightly oversized or have a wavy edge.

13. Now you can plan your layout! Drawing from all three sets of blocks, begin laying out a basketweave setting, alternating horizontal and vertical orientation across the first row of 10 blocks. Rotate or switch blocks as you go to achieve lots of light and dark movement.

14. Lay out the second row of blocks with opposite alignment, so that horizontal goes under vertical and vice versa. Continue to lay out eight rows with 10 blocks across each.

15. Mix and match blocks, rotate them, or change placement to keep the color variety dynamic, without too much dark or light pooling anywhere. The improvisational nature of the layout makes it interesting!

16. When you are happy with your layout, take a photo for reference. Look at that, too, for a slightly different perspective.

17. Label slips of paper or Post-it Notes 1–8, and pin them to the upper left corner of the leftmost block in each row. Take one more photo with the labels showing for reference.

ASSEMBLE THE QUILT TOP

18. Working from left to right, assemble each row, joining blocks with a ⅓-in. seam allowance. Leave all pinned-row labels on.

19. When you've assembled each row, divide them into odd and even stacks and press all odd row seams to the left and even to the right (or alternate as you choose).

20. Join rows 1 + 2, 3 + 4, 5 + 6, and 7 + 8 with a ⅓-in. seam allowance, pinning at seamlines and nesting seams.

21. Now join rows 1 + 2 to 3 + 4 and rows 5 + 6 to 7 + 8 in the same way. You now have two halves of your quilt, ready to be joined in the middle.

22. Press the back of section 1–4 with light spray starch, pressing the row-joining seams away from the center. Press the seams of section 5–8 away from the center. Then press the front of both sections. This is quick pressing, since the blocks are so simple.

23. Pin or sew over the pressed seam allowances, then topstitch all row seams in both sections, catching all pressed seams with your stitching. This gives the quilt top a cohesiveness and flow.

24. Carefully pinning each seamline and nesting seams, join the two sections, the top and bottom of the quilt top, together at the centerline with a ⅓-in. seam allowance. Press the seam downward, press the front of the quilt, and topstitch over that final seam to finish your quilt top.

FINISH THE QUILT

25. Arrange the quilt top over the batting and baste them together. This is an unusual project in that you do not baste the top two layers to the quilt back, since you want the laminated cotton to stay waterproof.

26. Machine- or hand-tie at the center of each block to join the quilt top to the batting. Trim all threads. Stitch around the perimeter, and square it up to trim excess batting.

27. Arrange the laminated cotton, right side down, and place the quilt top over it, right side up. Align edges and corners and trim any excess backing. Pin in place around the perimeter, then stitch the perimeter with a long basting machine stitch to secure the three layers.

28. Fold and press the webbing following the manufacturer's guidelines, using a warm—not hot—iron and pressing cloth. If you need to join two sections, zigzag them together with ends touching rather than sewing a bulky seam.

29. Pin on the binding, easing pins through the thick webbing and laminated back. Stitch it down around the perimeter, starting at the very beginning of the folded binding and following the machine-binding instructions (but do not leave an open section). Baste at the corners.

30. When you reach the beginning of the binding, layer the working binding over the first seam and trim it to a ⅓-in. overlap. Stitch it down just as you would a joined binding. Then reinforce the overlap section with a zigzag stitch to secure it.

flying in pairs quilt

Finished block size (one paired set of triangles): 5 in. wide x 4½ in. high
Finished size: 38 in. wide x 36 in. high
Longarm quilted by Nancy Stovall in a horizontal lines pattern
Seam allowance: ¼ in.

AT 5 IN. SQUARE, CHARM SQUARES ARE A LOVELY size for patchwork, but they really shine in half-square triangle (HST) blocks. For this quilt, I chose a charm pack of Shimmer On coordinates in Robert Kaufman's Essex Linen for a gorgeous, rich palette and a very modern wall quilt. The piecing was quick and fun, but the layout was my favorite part — arranging and rearranging the beautiful pairs of triangles until the movement and feel of them together was just right.

WHAT YOU'LL NEED

- Sewing + Quilting Kit (pp. 10–13)
- 32 charm squares, two each of 16 colors; I used the Shimmer On coordinates from Essex Linen Collection by Robert Kaufman; or cut your own fabrics to 5 in. square
- 1 yd. of neutral linen or other background fabric; I used Essex Champagne
- Batting measuring 40 in. x 42 in.
- Backing measuring 40 in. x 42 in.
- ¼ yd. of fabric for binding, or 162 in./4½ yd. of ½-in. double-fold binding tape

cutting key	A (assorted Essex Linens)	B (Essex Champagne)
HST blocks	Thirty-two 5-in. squares, two from each of 16 fabrics	Thirty-two 5-in. squares
Horizontal sashing		Three 1-in. x WOF strips
Vertical sashing		Three 1½-in. x WOF strips
Borders		Four 2-in. x WOF strips
Backing	40 in. x 42 in. (I used Kona champagne quilting cotton)	
Binding	Four 2-in. x WOF strips (I used Kona tan quilting cotton)	

techniques used

Pressing, *pp. 24–25*

Cutting, *pp. 25–26*

2-at-a-time
HST method, *pp. 42–43*

Assembling
a quilt, *p. 50*

Sashing, *p. 52*

Borders, *pp. 45–46*

Binding, *pp. 47–49*

If you're quilting this
project at home, you'll
also baste, mark, and
quilt, *pp. 53–55*

HERE'S MY ADVICE

Using solids or nondirectional fabrics for the triangles/
geese is crucial; the 2-at-a-time method uses opposing
fabric grain settings in the finished paired triangles, so
an obvious print or fabric weave may appear broken.
With solids, the effect is very subtle, almost impossible
to see within the whole design.

CUTTING + PIECING

1. Cut and press all fabrics you'll use to construct the blocks (see the Cutting Key). It is easiest to cut the background squares if you first cut four 5-in. x WOF strips, then subcut those into eight 5-in. squares each.

2. Press all cut squares and charm squares with light spray starch. Using the 2-at-a-time method, piece 64 HST blocks, pressing and trimming them to make 4½-in. blocks; press seams toward the solid/darker fabric.

3. Join 2 HST blocks at a time to form the triangles, matching and pinning color and seam angles carefully and stitching with a ¼-in. seam allowance. Press the seam open so it lies flat. Repeat to make 32 flying geese, 2 each of 16 colors.

4. Join each pair of same-color geese triangle blocks into one unit, pressing the seam up toward the higher block of the two. Press all blocks and square up the sides if any are not straight.

5. Now lay out the 16 block pairs in the design shown, with the first and third columns of triangles pointing up, and the second and fourth pointing down. Move blocks around until you like the color mix and movement. Take a photo for reference.

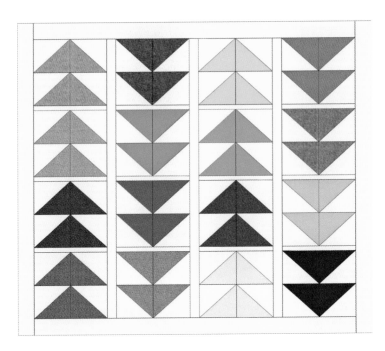

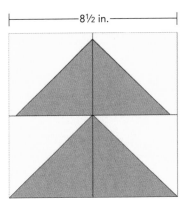

8½ in.

ASSEMBLE THE QUILT TOP

6. You'll assemble this quilt top in columns instead of rows. Label the leftmost column 1, the next one 2, and so on, pinning slips of paper on the top block of each column. Take one last photo and stack the blocks in each column from top down.

7. Begin joining the 4 paired-triangle blocks in column 1, working from top to bottom, by adding a 1-in. strip of horizontal sashing between each. Trim the sashing strips flush with the blocks' edges, and press seams toward the sashing.

8. Repeat to join the blocks in columns 2, 3, and 4 with 1-in. sashing. Press all seams toward the sashing.

9. Now join columns 1 + 2 and then columns 3 + 4, using 1½-in. vertical sashing. Press all seams toward the sashing, and trim the top and bottom of the quilt top flush with the blocks' edges.

10. Join a strip of 2-in. border fabric to first the top and then the bottom of the quilt top, pressing seams away from the center and toward the border. Repeat to add a 2-in. border strip to the left and right sides. Press the quilt top on both the right and wrong sides.

FINISH THE QUILT

11. My quilt was longarm-quilted in a pattern of horizontal lines, spaced ¼ in. apart, which is also very achievable on a home machine. If you are quilting this project yourself, mark the quilt top with quilting lines with chalk, a fabric pen, or painter's tape. For something as simple as straight lines, mark the centerline with tape for reference.

12. Layer the quilt top, batting, and backing, then baste.

make it simpler

Make Flying in Pairs as a mini quilt using just
9 charm squares in different colors (no repeats)
and ⅓ yd. of background linen. Using the 4-at-a-
time HST method (p. 44), make 36 HSTs from
nine sets of assorted charm squares and 5-in.
background fabric squares, trimming them to
3-in. squares.

  Join two HSTs at a time into flying geese
triangles until you have 18, and pair those to
create 9 double-triangle blocks. Assemble
a 3-block x 3-block layout of flying geese,
joining each pair into columns of three, with 1-in.
horizontal sashing; then join the columns with 1½-in.
vertical sashing. Add 1-in. borders on all four sides (left
and right sides first, then top and bottom), then press. I
chose a design of horizontal lines spaced ½ in. apart, very
similar to my original version, and marked them two or
three at a time with washi tape from the center outward.
Baste, hand- or machine quilt, and bind. Your finished mini
will measure 19 in. x 17 in.

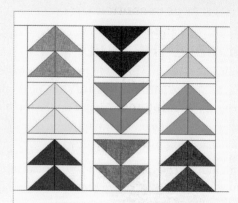

take it further

Continue this design to piece a minimalist bed quilt, using
50 charm squares to yield 25 pairs of flying geese triangles
arranged in a 5 x 5 layout, or 72 charm squares to yield 36 pairs
in a 6 x 6 layout, and so on. Add generous borders on all sides,
so the design floats within negative space.

13. Start quilting at the center, following the edge of
your first horizontal line of tape, and work above and
below to fill your quilt. Measure down and move your
tape line to the next increment as you go, checking
with a ruler to make sure the lines are straight and
adjusting if need be.

14. After quilting is complete, stitch the perimeter
of the quilt, trim excess batting and backing, and
machine-bind. I used a tan quilting cotton rather
than linen for my handmade binding, since lighter-
weight cotton folds much more easily.

sunlight baby quilt

Finished block size: 7½ in. square
Finished size: 38 in. x 38 in.
Longarm quilted by Nancy Stovall in a hexagon pattern
Seam allowance: ¼ in.

THIS SWEET BABY QUILT UPDATES THE VERY TRADITIONAL Barn Raising log cabin block setting by elevating the focal-point diamond and moving it off center, as well as mixing pops of contrasting color and texture into the dark-and-light blocks here and there. Using a soft recessive neutral like light gray lets the celebratory soft yellow sections of the design shine and radiate. And chain-piecing means these blocks come together very quickly.

WHAT YOU'LL NEED

- Sewing + Quilting Kit (pp. 10–13)

- 1¼ yd. total of dominant fabrics; I used 1 yd. of Michael Miller Cotton Couture in Canary, with about ¼ yd. of two Heather Ross honeybee prints and a few scraps of yellow crosshatch as contrast

- ¾ yd. total of recessive fabrics; I used ⅔ yd. of Cotton Couture in Fog, with ⅛ yd. of a subtle Japanese gray and white print

- Batting measuring 42 in. x 42 in.

- Backing measuring 42 in. x 42 in.

- ¼ yd. of fabric for binding, or 162 in./4½ yd. of ½-in. double-fold binding tape; I used the same honeybee print

cutting key	A (dominant fabrics)	B (recessive fabrics)
Log cabin blocks	Seventeen 2-in. x WOF strips (includes center squares)	Eleven 2-in. x WOF strips
Binding	Four 2-in. x WOF strips	
Backing	42 in. x 42 in. (can be pieced)	

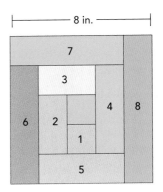

CUTTING + PIECING

1. Cut and press all fabrics you'll use to construct the 25 blocks (see the Cutting Key).

2. To begin the blocks, align one strip of dominant color A (yellow) and one strip of recessive color B (gray). With right sides facing, stitch them together the entire length of the strips with a ¼-in. seam allowance along one long edge, holding them together so they feed through evenly and stay aligned (you can pin if you'd like to, but remove the pins as you approach them). Press the long seam toward the gray side.

3. Using a quilt ruler and rotary cutter, cut the joined strips into 2-in. lengths. These will be your yellow centers, each with a first gray log. Depending on the width of your fabric, you should have about 20 center + log 1 pairs.

4. Count the number of centers you still need (for example, if you have 20, you'll need 5 more), and cut a 2-in. strip of each color to that needed length (5 centers x 2-in. length = 10 in.) from your cut strips. Now sew these two shorter strips together, and repeat to press and cut them into center + log 1 pairs. You should now have 25 total.

5. Chain-piece to add a second log in color B to each of the 25 center + log 1 pairs, always working in a clockwise direction as you piece. Feel free to mix the complementary recessive fabric into a few of them. Cut and press the units. You will now have completed the first side (recessive) of each block's first tier, with both seams pressed toward the logs.

6. Switch to color A (dominant fabrics), and chain-piece to add log 3 to the pieced units. When you reach the end of a strip of color A, or whenever you like, you can use a same-color print strip for the next log in some of these blocks, then press and cut all units. Note: You'll need to use multiple strips to add logs for each of the chain-piecing rounds now, so feel free to mix in strips of same-color prints. I like to use a contrast print only once in each block, but it's totally up to you!

7. Repeat step 6 to add a yellow log 4; press and cut the units apart. You've now finished the first tier and should have 25 cute little mini-blocks! Press the back and front, then square up.

8. Following the previous instructions, add logs 5 and 6 in recessive gray solid/prints to border the gray inner tier, and then logs 7 and 8 in dominant yellow solid/prints to border the yellow inner tier. Press and square up.

ASSEMBLE THE QUILT TOP

9. Now comes the fun part: deciding on your block layout. Arrange the blocks on a design wall, floor, tabletop, or neutral-colored flannel in a 5-block x 5-block layout. You can follow my diagram for an off-center Barn Raising or rotate the blocks to try any (or all) of the other log cabin layouts before you decide on a final design.

10. Once you like the setting, look to see if your prints and pops of contrast fabrics are "pooling" too much—appearing close together instead of mixing into other areas of mostly solids. Take a photo to see the potential contrasts more sharply. Rearrange blocks until you like the movement and variety within the layout. Once you are happy with the layout, take a photo for reference.

11. Label the rows 1–5, and pin a numbered label on the leftmost block in each row. Take one last photo for reference. Make a neat stack of each row, from left to right, and assemble the rows one by one. With right sides facing, join each block to its neighbor with a ¼-in. seam allowance.

12. Press odd-number row seams to the left (1, 3, 5) and even-number rows to the right (2, 4).

make it simpler

Use just two contrast fabrics, A and B, instead of mixing in other fabrics for texture.

take it further

Make a mini version using a mix of deeper-hued coral prints and add hand-quilting or any other special finishing details. For this smaller variation, all blocks are the same size and pieced the same way as the Sunlight version but use a larger variety of fabrics. The mini is a 9-block/3 x 3 grid layout, measuring 23 in. square.

13. Nesting seams, pin the bottom of row 1 to the top of row 2, being sure to pin at each block's row seam. Stitch rows 1 and 2 together, checking to make sure the blocks line up neatly.

14. Repeat to join the bottom of row 2 to the top of row 3. Then join the bottom of row 4 to the top of row 5. Press all row seams away from the center.

15. Finish your quilt top by pinning and stitching the upper section (rows 1–3) to the lower section (rows 4 and 5). Press seams away from the center.

FINISH THE QUILT

16. You can hand- or machine-quilt, tie, or finish your baby quilt any way you like. I collaborated with longarm quilter Nancy Stovall, who quilted mine with a charming honeycomb pattern of hexagons. If you are quilting your quilt, mark quilting lines with chalk, a fabric pen, or painter's tape.

17. Layer the quilt top, batting, and backing, then baste. Quilt or tie as desired, following your marked lines or tape. Stitch the perimeter and trim away excess backing and batting.

18. After quilting or tying is complete, stitch the perimeter and trim excess backing and batting. Prepare handmade binding from fabric, or use premade ½-in. double-fold binding to machine-bind your quilt.

HERE'S MY ADVICE

Use the color placement in the Sunlight Baby Quilt diagram as inspiration for mixing pops of contrasting color into dominant and recessive color palettes, not as an exact layout to follow carefully. If I made a second version, it would have its own scrappy charm, with no two blocks exactly alike even though they use the same very simple design.

sunset mini-quilt

1. First cut six 2-in. x WOF strips of the assorted dominant color prints (corals) and four 2-in. x WOF strips of the assorted recessive color (grays). Trim all selvages.

2. Cut a 6-in. strip of each of three coral prints, and chain-piece to join each of them to a strip of gray. Press and trim into nine 2-in. center + log 1 pairs, measuring 2 in. square as a unit. Add a gray log 2 to all blocks, then add a coral log 3 to all blocks, either one at a time or by chain-piecing. I chose not to repeat coral fabrics within a block, so I used five different prints in each one. Add a coral log 4 to each block, then press and square up. Continue piecing a second tier of logs in the same way, varying the print fabrics as much as you like. Press and square up.

3. Lay out the blocks in a 3 x 3 arrangement, moving them around for color mix. Take a photo and mark each row with a pinned label. Join rows 1–3, then pin the rows together, matching block seams. Press the quilt top back and front.

4. Mark for quilting. I chose to stitch my block seams in the ditch, then added a crosshatch of diagonal machine-quilting lines. I also hand-quilted all around the diamond shapes with matching coral perle cotton.

5. Finish the mini-quilt by layering the quilt top, batting, and backing; bind to complete.

pinwheels baby quilt

Finished block size: 10 in. x 10 in.
Finished size: 40 in. x 40 in.
Longarm quilted by Nancy Stovall in a butterfly pattern
Seam allowance: ¼ in.

I LOVE 1950S, '60S, AND '70S VINTAGE SHEETS—THE FUN prints and lively colors are such a joy to use in patchwork and quilting projects. I chose all yellow, blue, and green patterns for this palette, since the summery mix felt perfect for a lighthearted baby quilt. Pinwheels using 4-at-a-time HST blocks are quick and easy to piece together and bring freshness and energy to the super-soft, nostalgic prints scattered throughout. Of course, you can use modern quilting cotton prints or solids instead, if you like.

My PMQG friend Kelly Cole has a wonderful shop, Vintage Fabric Studio, that sells precut 8½-in. squares in a huge variety of prints, which is the size I started with for my blocks. You can start there to choose a gorgeous variety of precuts, find vintage sheets at garage sales or thrift stores, or swap with friends. You can also find fat-quarter (FQ) cuts of many vintage sheets in Kelly's shop or from Etsy sellers and cut your own squares from those.

WHAT YOU'LL NEED

- Sewing + Quilting Kit (pp. 10–13)

- Sixteen 8½-in. squares—two each of eight prints for this design. Cut from yardage, scraps, or FQs, or buy precuts in this size.

- 1 twin flat or fitted vintage or new sheet in a subtle print (I chose a soft green with butterflies) for cutting sixteen 8½-in. squares of background fabric plus backing, or use a combination of two sheets

OR

- 1 yd. of 40-in.-wide print fabric for the background and 1¼ yd. for the backing (will include selvages instead of trimming them as usual)

- Batting measuring 44 in. x 44 in.

- ⅓ yd. of fabric for binding, or 171 in./4¾ yd. of ½-in. double-fold binding tape

techniques used

Pressing, *pp. 24–25*
Cutting, *pp. 25–26*
4-at-a-time HST method, *p. 44*
Quilt assembly, *p. 50*
Binding, *pp. 47–49*
If you're quilting this project at home, you'll also baste, mark, and quilt, *pp. 53–55*

109

cutting key	A (assorted pinwheel prints)	B (subtle background prints)	C (solid quilting cotton)
HST blocks	Sixteen 8½-in. squares—2 from each of the eight prints	Ten 3-in. x 60-in. strips	Ten 3-in. x 60-in. strips
Backing	44-in. x 44-in. piece	Sixteen 8½-in. squares	
Binding			Four and one-half 2-in. x WOF strips

CUTTING + PIECING

1. Cut and press all fabrics you'll use to construct the blocks and quilt (see the Cutting Key).

2. Press all squares. Using the 4-at-a-time HST method, make 64 HST blocks and press and trim them to 5½ in. square each.

3. Arrange the HST blocks into color-coordinated sets of 4, and lay out the first set in a pinwheel setting. With right sides facing, pin then stitch the top two blocks, matching seams and colors, and press the seams to the left. Join the bottom two blocks the same way, pressing the seams to the right. Now join the top and bottom blocks, nesting seams, pinning at the seamlines where colors meet, and stitching with a ¼-in. seam allowance.

make it simpler

Use just two favorite prints instead of eight in your pinwheels.

take it further

Create a larger bed quilt by continuing this lively, colorful design. Sixty-four pinwheel blocks would yield an 80-in.-square quilt. Make it completely scrappy or use favorite solids or prints for an intentional design.

4. Repeat to assemble 15 more pinwheels. You'll now have two each of 8 print pinwheel blocks. Press, trim, and square up the 16 blocks so they measure 10½ in. square.

ASSEMBLE THE QUILT TOP

5. Arrange the blocks in a 4 x 4 layout, moving them around until you like the color and print mix. I chose to separate the identical pinwheels, with one each on the top and bottom half of the quilt. When you like the layout, take a photo.

6. Label the rows 1–4, and pin a numbered label on the leftmost block in each row.

7. With right sides facing, pin the first row of pinwheel blocks together, working from left to right. Pin at the top, center, and bottom seam matches for a neat join, and stitch them together using a ¼-in. seam allowance.

8. Repeat to join rows 2, 3, and 4. Press the backs of each row, pressing seams to one side—odd rows (1 and 3) to the left and even (2 and 4) to the right.

 HERE'S MY ADVICE

It will be obvious if block seams don't match up, so check the angle lines and corners when you've finished sewing. If you missed one, simply seam-rip, repin, and resew.

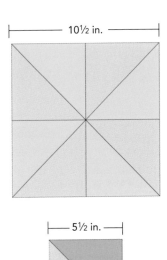

10½ in.

5½ in.

9. Pin rows 1 + 2 together, nesting seams and matching block edges. Sew with a ¼-in. seam allowance. Repeat to join rows 3 + 4. Join the two halves of the quilt with a ¼-in. seam allowance. Press your quilt top front and back.

FINISH THE QUILT

10. If you are quilting this project at home, mark your quilt top for quilting using chalk, a fabric pen, or painter's tape. Layer the quilt top, batting, and backing, and quilt as desired.

11. Stitch the perimeter of your quilt, then trim away excess batting and backing.

12. Prepare handmade binding from fabric, or use premade ½-in. double-fold binding to machine-bind your quilt.

HERE'S MY ADVICE

If you are working with a longarm quilter, collaborate with them to choose a design. Nancy Stovall and I came up with a fun, lighthearted pattern of butterflies and loops.

memento mini-quilts

Finished block size (one HST): 2½ in. square
Finished size: 17 in. x 17 in.
Machine outline quilted with contrast hand quilting
Seam allowance: ¼ in.

I ALWAYS WANTED TO MAKE SPECIAL MEMENTO QUILTS FOR my kids, imagining I'd piece one block a year in their favorite colors, then put all of them together to finish as they grew up. I made one for my daughter's first birthday, and then as things sped along, I found myself with two children and no every-year-block quilts coming together for either of them!

So I came up with a new plan. I sorted through fabric scraps left over from things I made each of them over the years, from my son's baby quilt to the dress my daughter wore on the first day of fourth grade. I cut charm squares of our favorites and then pieced all of them into a variety of tiny HST blocks. Arranging the triangles into a beautiful, simple layout brought those sweet handmade pieces back to life in a brand-new way.

Use this idea however you'd like—round up special scraps like I did or dip into a favorite fabric collection or color palette that reminds you of who you're celebrating. Best of all, this project actually makes enough blocks for *four* mini-quilts—maybe one for a child, one for the parents, and two more for grandparents or special family friends. With HSTs, the layout options are endless, so you can make them all the same or change the design for each recipient.

WHAT YOU'LL NEED
(for 4 mini quilts)

- Sewing + Quilting Kit (pp. 10–13)

- 24 charm squares (5-in. squares) of assorted fabrics that are special to you

- 1¼ yd. of background fabric; I used crosshatch patterns in a soft complementary color for both of my mini-quilts

- Batting measuring 18 in. x 18 in. per quilt (1 yd. total)

- Backing measuring 18 in. x 18 in. quilt (1 yd. total); I used one of my favorite prints for each back

- ⅛ yd. per quilt for binding (½ yd. total) or 81 in./2¼ yd. prepared ½-in. double-fold binding per quilt

techniques used

Pressing, *pp. 24–25*
Cutting, *pp. 25–26*
4-at-a-time HST method, *p. 44*
Quilt assembly, *p. 50*
Outline quilting, *p. 53*
Hand-quilting, *p. 55*
Binding, *pp. 47–49*
If you're quilting this project at home, you'll also baste, mark, and quilt, *pp. 53–55*

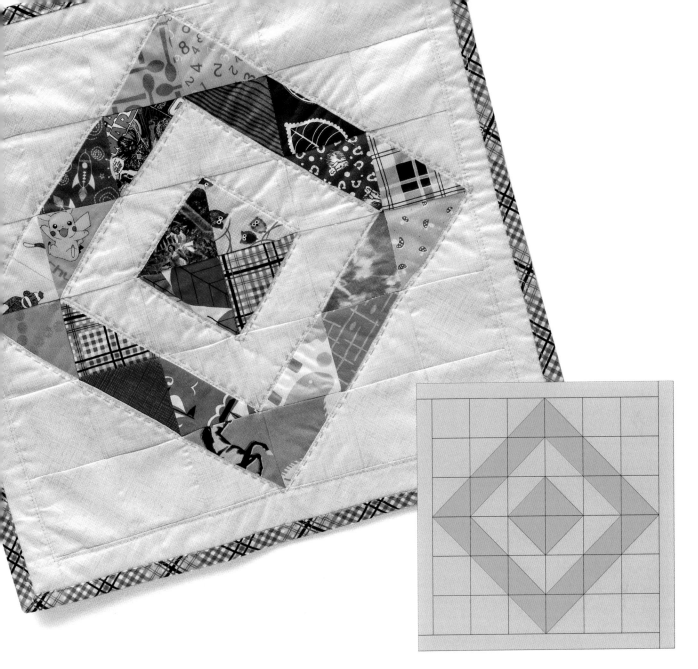

cutting key	**A** (assorted fabrics)	**B** (background fabric)
HST blocks	Twenty-four 5-in. charm squares	Twenty-four 5-in. charm squares
Background		Forty-eight 3-in. squares (twelve for each mini)
Borders		Eight 1½-in. x WOF strips (two for each mini)
Backing	Four 18-in. squares (one for each mini)	
Binding	Eight 2-in. x WOF strips (two for each mini)	

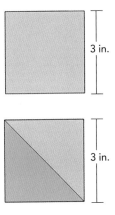

3 in.

3 in.

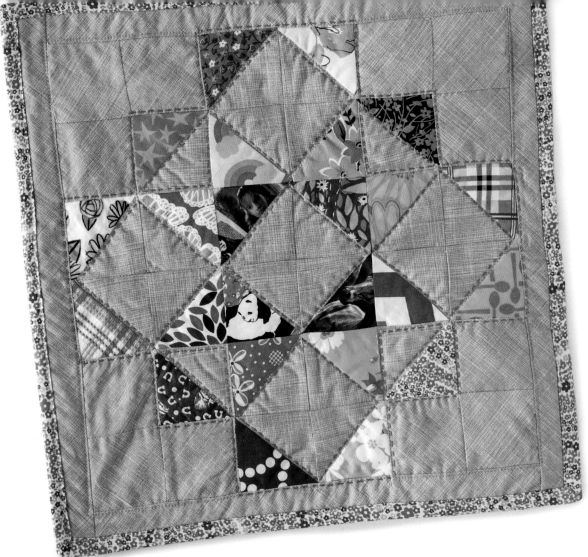

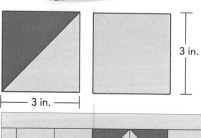

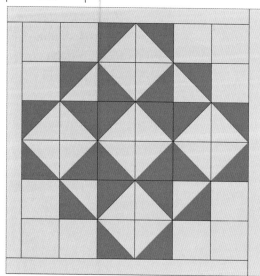

CUTTING + PIECING

1. Cut all of the 5-in. and 3-in. squares according to the Cutting Key on p. 113, then press. Press the border strips and set aside.

 HERE'S MY ADVICE

The easiest way to cut the background fabric into squares is to first cut it into strips. For the 5-in. squares, cut three 5-in. WOF strips of fabric, then cut each strip into eight 5-in. squares. For the 3-in. background squares, cut four 3-in. x WOF strips, then cut twelve 3-in. squares from each strip.

2. Using the 4-at-a-time HST method, pair the 24 prints and background fabric squares, and make them into a total of 96 mini HST blocks. After you cut them, press and trim into 3-in. HST blocks. You can

114

either press and trim one of each print (24) to make one quilt or prepare all 96 at the same time (for four quilts).

3. Choose the layout for your mini-quilt. I've included two that use a 6 x 6 grid of 24 HST blocks and 12 background squares: a simple, striking diamond with lots of negative space, and a sawtooth star with more intricacy, but you can play with your own layout ideas, too. Position the HSTs all around the layout until you like the flow and placement. I placed four special fabrics in the center of each design, then arranged the others from there. Fill in spaces with 3-in. squares, as shown in the diagrams.

4. Once you are happy with your design, take a photo, then label the rows 1–6 by pinning slips of paper on the leftmost block. Take one more photo.

ASSEMBLE THE QUILT TOP

5. With right sides facing and working from left to right, stitch the blocks in each row together with a ¼-in. seam allowance. When you have finished all

6 rows, press the seams to one side: odd rows (1, 3, 5) to the left and even (2, 4, 6) to the right. Press the front of the rows as well.

6. Pin rows 1 + 2 together, matching block edges and nesting seams. Stitch with a ¼-in. seam allowance.

7. Repeat to join rows 3 + 4, then 5 + 6. Join the three row sections the same way. Press all joining seams away from the center—upward or downward, with the rows 3 + 4 center seam pressed downward. Press the front of the quilt top.

8. Stitch the 1½-in. border strips to first the top and then the bottom edge, and then to both sides of the quilt top, pressing seams toward the borders each time.

FINISH THE QUILT

9. Mark the quilt top for quilting; if you are using a simple outline pattern like mine that follows block lines, you may not need to mark. Baste the quilt top, batting, and backing together.

10. Quilt as desired. I machine-quilted to outline the geometric pattern of the diamond and the sawtooth star designs using a matching thread and working from the center outward.

11. Add hand-quilting if you like. I used a contrast color of perle cotton to add a running-stitch embellishment all around my machine-quilting.

12. Stitch the perimeter, then trim away excess batting and backing.

13. Cut two 2-in. x WOF strips of fabric and make them into binding, or use prepared ½-in. double-fold binding to machine-bind your mini-quilt.

14. Add a special label for the recipient!

Note: To finish the other three mini-quilts, complete any additional background and border cutting by following the Cutting Key (p. 113). Lay out your mini-quilts however you'd like.

make it simpler

Use precut 5-in. charm squares from a favorite fabric collection or solids in colors you especially love for a simpler, equally beautiful mini-quilt.

take it further

Make a very special set of memento quilts with contributions from friends or family. Ask everyone to send you charm squares (5-in. squares) of favorite fabrics, for a total of 24. Combine all of them into the HST blocks for your mini-quilts. You could also make a larger wall quilt with all 96 HST blocks in one design.

mt. hood memento quilt

Block size: 60 in. x 45 in.
Finished size: 59 in. x 44 in.
Topstitched and perimeter-stitched
Seam allowance: ½ in

THE COLOR PALETTE OF THIS SIMPLE, COZY WOOL QUILT WAS inspired by beautiful Mt. Hood here in Oregon. This spare, elongated take on the rail fence pattern, using just a few fabrics and the simplest of topstitching lines, is the perfect way to let the gorgeous jacquard designs shine. Whether your quilt is inspired by nature, a special trip, or simply colors you love, its warmth and meaning make it one you'll reach for all winter long.

Depending on the measurements of your wool blanket header, yardage, or reclaimed blankets, and how many pieces you use, your finished quilt may be a different size than mine. I've written these instructions for 60-in.-wide fabrics, but use them as a jumping-off point if your fabrics are different widths or lengths. The important thing is to mix colors and designs as you like best and to sew a sturdy, durable, and beautiful quilt that makes you happy whenever you see it.

WHAT YOU'LL NEED

- Sewing + Quilting Kit (pp. 10–13)
- Assorted blanket-weight wool fabrics: I used five fabrics between 3 in. and 5 in. wide and 60 in. long for a total of 11 strips
- Backing measuring 4 in. wider and taller than your quilt top; I used a 64-in. x 49-in. piece of lightweight worsted wool apparel fabric

techniques used

Pressing, *pp. 24–25*
Cutting, *pp. 25–26*
Rail fence piecing, *pp. 38–39*
Topstitching, *p. 27*
Clipping corners, *p. 29*
Edgstitching, *p. 27*

 HERE'S MY ADVICE

The Pendleton Woolen Mill Store in Portland, where I found all my fabrics, sells Pendleton blanket header scraps as well as yardage for mail order around the world. You can also cut up any kind of old wool blankets from estate sales, thrift stores, or surplus stores, cutting strips away from any moth holes or worn places. If you need to join multiple pieces to achieve the overall width needed, simply sew with a ½-in. seam allowance end to end, press seams to one side, and topstitch to catch all layers. Then use that patchwork section as a single fabric.

117

cutting key	A (assorted wool blanket-weight fabrics)	B (lightweight wool backing fabric)
Rail fence block	3-in. to 5-in. x 60-in. strips (I used 11 total pieces of blanket header, in five different fabrics)	
Backing		64 in. x 49 in.—can be pieced

CHOOSING FABRIC + PIECING

1. Choose your wool fabrics, arranging them in folds to see how they look together. You can use as few as 2 and as many as 11 (or more) in this design. Check your fabric for damage and make sure the sections are similar widths—mine were all at least 60 in. wide. If you have narrower sections, you can join two together (see "Here's My Advice" on p. 116), and if some are wider, trim them down to the same measurement.

2. Decide on the overall layout order of the fabrics, working from top to bottom. I auditioned several ideas and took lots of photos before deciding on a simple, symmetrical arrangement of five fabrics—one in the center, with five more strips radiating outward, including a repeat of the center fabric. See the diagram above for a clearer look at my design. I used one sky blue that reminded me of Trillium Lake and several deep forest greens and browns. All of my fabric strips measured between 3 in. and 5 in. wide, but you can use strips that are all the

same measurement if you prefer. I don't recommend going much narrower than 3 in. since a piece that small will start to disappear in a design. You can match any center designs within your different fabrics if you like.

3. Using a rotary cutter and quilt ruler, trim all strips so they are the same length across, and their long edges are straight and on grain.

4. Take a final photo when you are happy with your design. Now label each strip with a numbered slip of paper (1–11 for my quilt), pinning it to the left end of each strip, and take a photo of that, too.

5. Working from the center strip (6) outward, pin the center strip to the one just above it (5). You can pin from edge to edge if the strips are all solids or the same width, or match centers if you want to align beautiful jacquard patterns like mine.

6. Join strips 5 + 6 with a ½-in. straight seam and a longer stitch length. Press with a steam iron set to wool, using distilled water in a spray bottle if desired, so the seam is pressed to one side, away from center. Press the front of the joined strips, then pin all along the seam, catching all layers in the pins.

7. Topstitch along the seam, ⅛ in. to ¼ in. from the seamline, to secure the join and so the fabrics lie flat together, from one end to the other.

8. Join strip 4 to the top edge of 5 + 6, matching centers and pinning. Join with a ½-in. seam allowance, press, and topstitch as before.

9. Continue to join all strips, working upward, until you reach the top of the quilt, so strips 1–6 are joined. Set this section aside.

10. Join strips 7 + 8 the same way, matching centers and topstitching. Continue joining strips to this section until you reach strip 11, the bottom strip of the quilt.

11. Pin and stitch the top section of the quilt to the bottom section with a ½-in. seam allowance, matching centers and supporting the full weight of the quilt on your sewing table or a chair so it doesn't pull the seam out of alignment.

12. Carefully supporting the weight of the quilt, press, pin, and topstitch the final joining seam.

13. Square up the quilt, trimming any longer edges so it is straight and neat.

FINISH THE QUILT TOP

14. Now prepare the quilt backing. If you need to join several sections together to achieve a big enough piece, sew them with a ½-in. seam allowance, right sides facing. Press seams to one side and topstitch just as you did on the quilt top.

15. You'll use a simple perimeter stitching method instead of binding to finish this quilt. Lay the quilt back on a large, flat surface, right side up. Now lay your quilt top over it, right side down, and align the two layers so they're neat and the edges generally match. Pin all around the perimeter, leaving an 8-in. opening at the bottom. Carefully turn the pinned quilt over to check the back. If it's pulling, creased, or off grain, gently unpin that section, realign, and repin.

16. Using a longer straight stitch, start at one side of the opening and sew around the perimeter of the quilt, ½ in. from the edge of the top, stitching smoothly over the seams. Stop at the other side of the opening, leaving it unsewn. Check the back to make sure there are no tucks or uneven areas.

17. Trim excess backing and clip corners.

18. Turn the quilt right side out through the opening, shaking it gently so it settles smoothly. Ease the corners open so they are neat and square. Press all around the outer edges of the quilt and pin the perimeter neatly. Fold ½ in. of both layers to the inside of the quilt at the opening, and pin that securely, too. Pinning all four edges of the quilt will make sure it's neatly aligned for the final round of topstitching.

19. Using a longer stitch length, stitch around the perimeter of the quilt, closing the opening securely and backstitching at the beginning and end to secure the seam.

20. Press or simply shake out—your wool quilt is finished and ready to cuddle with!

make it simpler

Use just two wool blanket fabrics and alternate strips for a symmetrical pattern, or vary widths within your design for more unexpectedness.

take it further

Make a special milestone quilt using this basic design. I made my in-laws, Paul and Nancy, a special Golden Anniversary quilt out of just two Pendleton wool fabrics, a striped serape and a jacquard cross pattern, but expanded the design a bit by adding vertical panels to each side so it was framed for more impact. I also hand-embroidered a special label on the front in perle cotton, with a "50" stitched inside a heart.

golden rays quilt

Finished block size: 7½ in. square
Finished size: 79 in. x 79 in.
Longarm quilted by Nancy Stovall in an allover circles pattern
Seam allowance: ¼ in.

MY EIGHT-YEAR-OLD SON, EVERETT, IS A BRIGHT, SWEET, AND funny kid, absorbed in a game one minute and telling jokes the next. His sunny personality and warmth is perfectly reflected in his favorite color. I made him a baby quilt in soft yellow sock-monkey flannel framed with deep wood-grain browns, and a toddler-sized play quilt in bright aquas and yellows. Now that he's growing up, I wanted to design a quilt he'd love for years, elevating the color palette a bit, too.

The radiant diagonals in string quilting felt just right for this quilt, and mixing dozens of prints and solids with one center golden focus fabric brought lots of movement. The finished quilt is as joyful and warm as he is. All the cutting, trimming, and pressing (beware—it's a lot!) was so worth it when I showed him the finished top and he ran toward me to hug it close.

This quilt would be wonderful with a totally different palette, too. Choose a focus fabric in a color you love and let it set the tone—navy would add crispness, white would feel fresh and light, and black presents as sleek and sophisticated. Or use all brights for an exuberant feel.

WHAT YOU'LL NEED

- Sewing + Quilting Kit (pp. 10–13), including 8-in.-square template with bias/diagonal marking

- 3 yd. of a focus fabric, solid or subtle; I used tonal metallic gold Pearl Bracelets by Lizzy House

- 3 yd. of muslin for foundation piecing

- A total of about 8 yd. of scraps, ¼-yd. cuts, or fat quarters (FQs) of a variety of prints and solids in supporting colors; I used 12 browns and 16 blues, mostly prints, plus 3 in gold/white for a bit of contrast, each about a quarter yard

- ⅔ yd. to ¾ yd. of border fabric; I used blue Pearl Bracelets

- Batting measuring 83 in. x 83 in.

- Backing measuring 83 in. x 83 in.

- ½ yd. of fabric for binding or 324 in./9 yd. of ½-in. double-fold binding tape; I used a wood-grain print

techniques used

Pressing, *pp. 24–25*

Cutting, *pp. 25–26*

String piecing, *pp. 40–41*

Sashing, *p. 52*

Borders, *pp. 45–46*

Binding, *pp. 47–49*

If you're quilting this project at home, you'll also baste, mark, and quilt, *pp. 53–55*

cutting key	Focus fabric	Supporting fabrics	Muslin
String blocks	Twenty to twenty-two 2-in. x WOF strips	30 quarter-yards or FQs of various prints and solids, cut into strips of varying widths, between 1 in. and 3 in. x WOF	
Foundation squares			Sixty-four 8-in. squares
Sashing	About thirty-two 2-in. x WOF strips		
Borders		Eight 3-in. x WOF strips cut from one of your contrast fabrics	
Binding		Four 2-in. x WOF strips cut from one of your contrast fabrics	
Backing		83-in. x 83-in. pieced or whole cloth fabric	

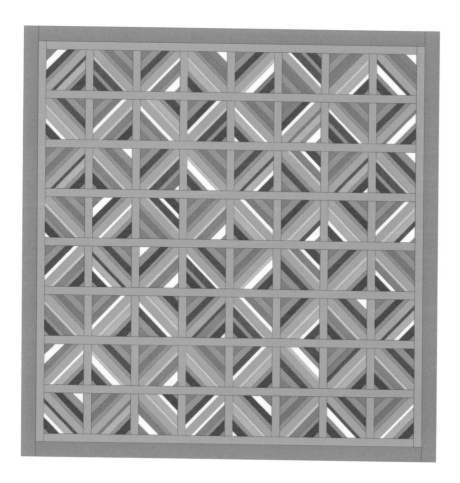

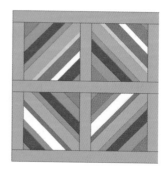

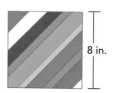

8 in.

Choose your focus fabric and then decide on two (or more) colors or shades that harmonize with it for your supporting fabrics. I like to fold or swatch fabrics together to get a sense of how they interact. Edit out anything that feels discordant or off. I think it's ideal to use anywhere from 15 to 30 prints and solids, but you can always start with a more limited number and then add in new prints as you go. Just be sure to limit strong directional prints, since block placement is so varied.

CUTTING + PIECING

1. Cut and press all fabrics following the Cutting Key. For the foundation blocks, it is easiest if you cut thirteen 8-in.-wide strips, then cut those into 5 squares each. For the string blocks, piece two leftover end strips together for the center diagonal of a new block to use fewer strips. Organize the strips by color family in zip-top bags or shallow boxes and stack your muslin blocks together.

HERE'S MY ADVICE

I like to cut my supporting fabric strips in different widths—one narrow 1-in. strip and one or two each of 1½-in., 2-in., and 2½-in. strips. There is no exact formula, so vary widths as desired.

2. Using the basic string block method (pp. 40–41), pin a strip of 2-in. focus fabric diagonally across the first foundation block, right side up. Position a contrast strip over it, and stitch down the right edge with a ¼-in. seam allowance. Now turn the block around, and align another contrast strip to the opposite side, stitching it down the same way. Trim longer strips and press.

3. Continue building the block using a variety of prints, widths, and colors. I mostly alternated colors, so the blues and browns moved around the blocks quite a bit. My recommendation is to include one 1-in. strip somewhere in each block for a striking

design—the narrow ½-in. finished strip looks great mixed in with the wider ones.

4. Finish the block by piecing strips to the corners and pressing the block. Set scraps and diagonal trim cuts aside—they are perfect for finishing future corners.

5. Piece 9 more blocks the same way, always starting with the same focus strip in the center and mixing in strips in different configurations—the more varied, the better.

6. Now press the first 10 blocks, flip them over so the wrong side is facing up, and use an 8-in. square template to trim them to perfect squares. Do not worry if your muslin squares have contracted a bit from all the stitching lines and some of the strip ends show around the edges—the blocks will be solidly constructed, and those small edge sections will disappear into the seam allowances.

7. Continue piecing blocks the same way to make a total of 64, then press and trim them all.

8. Place all 64 blocks in an 8 x 8 grid, forming 4 rows of 4 large diamonds each (see the diagram on the facing page). Leave a little space between them, since you'll sash these, but watch for nearby repeats or "pools" of color of light or dark that draw the eye too much. Move blocks around until you like the effect. Take a photo and look at that, too.

9. When you are happy with the layout, pin numbered tags 1-8 on the leftmost block of each row, and take a photo of that. Pick up stacks of the blocks in order, stacking 1-8 (these will be heavy, so move them carefully).

ASSEMBLE THE QUILT TOP

10. Working with the top row of blocks (row 1), join the blocks from left to right, placing a sashing strip in between each of them and trimming the strip flush with the blocks as you finish. You can use leftover strips from the center diagonals as sashing strips, too, as the width is the same. Be sure to leave the pinned tag on the leftmost block on each row.

11. Continue assembling rows 2–8 in the same way.

string quilting should be fun

There is a lot of cutting for this quilt, but you don't have to do it all at the same time. I planned and started cutting for this quilt in August, pieced 10 blocks, and then took a break to make several other quilts for the book. (I like to stop piecing after every 10 blocks and press and trim mine, but you can use any rhythm that feels right.) Then, in October, I cut more supporting fabrics and finished the other 54(!), making about 10 a day and rewatching *Downton Abbey* while I cut strips or trimmed blocks. This is a marathon, not a sprint, but it should be fun!

12. Press all rows, first on the wrong side and then on the right side, pressing seams toward the sashing.

13. Starting with the top row, assemble the quilt top by joining each row with a long strip of sashing. You'll need to sew two WOF strips together, using a ¼-in. seam allowance, to achieve the approximately 72-in. length needed for each full section of horizontal sashing. Moving paper labels if necessary (but repinning at the center of the block, out of the way of stitching), pin a long strip of sashing to the bottom edge of row 1, right sides facing. Sew it with a ¼-in. seam allowance, with the row as the top layer, so you can see the block seams and the sashing underneath. Trim the strip flush with the end of the row. If you have a partial strip left over, use it to join with the next section.

14. Pin the other edge of sashing to the top edge of row 2, right sides facing and matching edges, and stitch with a ¼-in. seam allowance. Press both seams toward the sashing. Set joined rows 1 + 2 aside.

15. Repeat the same process to join rows 3 + 4, 5 + 6, and 7 + 8. Press all row sections on both back and front.

16. Pin a long strip of sashing to the bottom edge of row 2 and stitch. Then stitch the top edge of row 3 to the other edge of the sashing. Press seams toward the sashing. Repeat to join rows 5 + 6 with 7 + 8.

17. Pin the bottom edge of row 4 to a long strip of sashing, working carefully, as the quilt top sections are now very heavy, and stitch together. Then pin the other edge of the sashing to the top of row 5, and carefully stitch those together. Press seams toward the sashing. You have finished the heart of your quilt!

18. Now join two WOF sashing strips together with a ¼-in. seam allowance four times, so you have 4 double-length strips. Pin and stitch the first long sashing strip to the top edge of the quilt top, pinning and sewing carefully, and trimming the extra length flush with the quilt top. Stitch the second strip to the bottom edge of the quilt top the same way. Press seams toward the sashing.

HERE'S MY ADVICE

The exposed sides of the string blocks with raw-edge bias fabric strips can be delicate and stretch out of alignment by the weight of the quilt top. Adding this outer tier of cross-grain sashing as an inner border really helps stabilize the entire design.

19. Add double-length sashing strips to the left and right edges of the quilt top, pressing seams toward the sashing.

20. Join two contrast fabric border strips together with a ¼-in. seam allowance four times, so you have 4 double-length strips. Pin and stitch the first border strip to the top edge of the sashing, then add the second border strip to the bottom edge. Press seams toward the border. Now stitch the third and fourth border strips to the left and right edges of the quilt top. Press seams toward the border, then press the front of the quilt top.

FINISH THE QUILT

21. Mark your quilt top for quilting, using chalk, a fabric pen, or painter's tape. Layer the quilt top, batting, and backing, and quilt as desired. Note: For a full-size quilt this heavy, I don't recommend hand- or machine-tying, or solely hand-quilting, as it is not as durable as sturdy machine-quilting.

22. If you are working with a longarm quilter, bring your unmarked quilt top, batting, and backing to her studio, and collaborate on a design.

23. When you have finished quilting, stitch the perimeter of your quilt, then trim away the excess batting and backing.

24. Prepare handmade binding from fabric, or use premade ½-in. double-fold binding to machine-bind your quilt.

25. Add a special label celebrating the child who's receiving your quilt. Find lots of ideas at sewplusquilt.com.

make it simpler

Use ¼ yd. to ½ yd. each of just 12 fabrics for supporting fabric strips instead of such a big variety, or simply reduce the size of the quilt to 6 x 6 blocks (for a total of 36 blocks instead of 64) and add wide borders to achieve a bed-size quilt.

take it further

Mix string blocks and solids for a striking half-square triangle design like this (see the Birthday Mini-Quilt on p. 144 for instructions).

bright star quilt

Finished block size: 7½ in. square
Finished size: 75 in. x 75 in.
Quilted by Nancy Stovall in a pearl bracelet-inspired pattern
Seam allowance: ¼ in.

MY 10-YEAR-OLD DAUGHTER, PEARL, LOVES COLOR, AND RAIN-bows are her favorite. For a quilt she could really grow up with, I pared down this palette for a pretty mix of vibrant pinks, purples, aquas, and corals. I balanced the brights with pale, low-volume light fabrics, including lots of soft vintage sheets with scattered florals.

Half-square triangles (HSTs) that balance lights and darks (or in this case, brights) create interesting angles and lines. After playing with layout options on Quilt Canvas, I chose a big, bright sawtooth star as the central motif, surrounded by a "bracelet" pattern radiating outward. The trick for this kind of detailed layout is to use more lights, which read as negative space, than brights, so neither overpowers the overall design.

Using the 2-at-a-time method of piecing HSTs means you'll have two exact duplicate blocks to mix within the quilt. Feel free to pair multiple squares of a favorite bright fabric with different light squares, so you have more variety throughout. This design uses only 8 total bright/bright blocks, including the central square of the star, so I chose to use really special fabric pairings for those, with prints I knew Pearl would especially love. I paired those with 8 fun assorted bright/light blocks to build the star's pretty points.

WHAT YOU'LL NEED

- Sewing + Quilting kit (pp.10–13), including 8½-in.- and 8-in.-square templates

- 4¼ yd. of assorted lights and 1⅔ yd. of assorted brights, or assorted scraps and fat quarters (FQs) of both light and bright low-volume prints

- Batting measuring 79 in. x 79 in.

- Backing measuring 79 in. x 79 in.; I used a vintage flat sheet with rainbows.

- ½ yd. of fabric for binding or 306 in./8½ yd. of prepared ½-in. double-fold binding tape; I used pink Pearl Bracelets by Lizzy House

techniques used

Pressing, *pp. 24–25*
Cutting, *pp. 25–26*
2-at-a-time HST method, *pp. 47–49*
Row assembly, *p. 50*
Binding, *pp. 47–49*
If you're quilting this project at home, you'll also baste, mark, and quilt, *pp. 53–55*

cutting key	Assorted light fabrics	Assorted bright fabrics
Sawtooth star and bracelet	Seventy-two 8½-in. squares	Twenty-eight 8½-in. squares
Backing	79 in. x 79 in. (can be pieced)	
Binding		Eight 2-in. x WOF strips

CUTTING + PIECING

1. Put all bright fabric squares into one stack or box and all lights into another. Begin by piecing four sets of bright squares together, using the 2-at-a-time method for HSTs (pp. 42–43). Cut, press, and trim them to 8 in. square. These **8 bright/bright HSTs** will make up the center of the star and the bigger "beads" on the bracelet radiating out from the design.

2. Now, piece bright/light HSTs, pairing compatible fabrics that harmonize but also show good contrast. You'll use the remaining 20 bright squares and 20 of the light squares. Use the 2-at-a-time method to make **40 bright/light HST blocks,** trimming them to 8 in. square.

3. Finally, organize the remaining 52 light squares into sets of twos to piece light/light HSTs the same way, making sure not to pair the same fabrics if you are using duplicates from the same print, creating **52 light/light HSTs.** Press and trim to 8 in. square.

4. Now arrange the quilt layout, starting with the center 4 x 4 grid that creates the star motif. Pay attention to the orientation of the center HST diagonals—for example, the 4 bright/bright blocks are set as a secondary diamond pattern rather than all being oriented the same way, and the sawtooth points radiate outward from there.

5. Once you have laid out the star, build out the design using light/light blocks. Place the blocks in a 10 x 10 grid, following the diagram for placing your bright/bright, bright/light, and light/light blocks. I arranged my duplicate bright/bright blocks diagonally across from their first placement in the star, as shown in the diagram above. The entire quilt design is symmetrical, and the light HST triangles

HERE'S MY ADVICE

Choose your light and bright fabrics, in any size from scraps to yardage, and "swatch" or stack them in separate piles. Take a photo of the options, filtering to black and white or using a Ruby Ruler or another color tool to see how they will read in a design. You want the lights to read calmly and brights to have more impact and depth. Put away any "medium"-reading fabrics for another project. Edit and arrange your fabrics until you like the mix, so there's plenty of variety in your brights especially, as those are the ones that will really pop in the finished quilt.

and blocks become the background to the bright star and bracelet designs.

6. Now begin building the "bracelet" of bright/light blocks around the center of the quilt, orienting the HST blocks as shown in the diagram.

7. Fill in the outer sections of the 10 x 10 grid with light/light and then bright/light blocks, working toward the corners.

8. Once the preliminary layout is set, take a photo. What do you see? Are there duplicates of exact fabrics or very similar colors near each other? Are any blocks misaligned? Move blocks around so you have a diverse, fun mix of fabrics throughout. Take photos as you go to evaluate each new setting. Be sure to filter them to black and white to check the values of colors as you go, and make sure the star and bracelet designs read clearly and boldly.

9. When you are happy with the layout, take a final photo for reference. Then, cut 20 slips of paper or Post-it Notes and label them 1A, 1B, and so on through 10A and 10B. Since this quilt has so many blocks, you will divide the design into quarters and build it in quadrants instead of full rows at once.

ASSEMBLE THE QUILT TOP

10. Pin 1A–10A slips to the leftmost block in each row, working top to bottom.

11. Now pin 1B–10B to the sixth block in each row—the second half of the quilt. Take another reference photo.

12. Stack all blocks in the 1A row, then 2A, 3A, 4A, and 5A, working left to right and top to bottom. Stack all 5 half rows in this upper left quadrant together, 25 blocks total.

take it further

13. Repeat for the 1B–5B rows, stacking those 5 half rows in the upper right quadrant together.

14. Repeat for the 6A–10A rows/lower left quadrant and 6B–10B rows/lower right quadrant, so you have 4 stacks of blocks, all labeled with their half-row slip.

15. Begin assembling the top, starting with the 1A quadrant. Join blocks in the 1A row, working from left to right and pinning, then stitching with a ¼-in. seam allowance. Then assemble row 2A, and so on, until the first 5 half rows are assembled.

16. Assemble the rows in each of the other quadrants: 1B–5B, 6A–10A, and 6B–10B.

17. Press seams in all odd rows (1A, 1B, 3A, 3B, etc.) toward the left side and in all even rows (2A, 2B, 4A, 4B, etc.) toward the right side.

18. Join all rows in the 1A quadrant, starting with 1A + 2A. Pin the blocks together, nesting seams, and matching angles and block-joining seams; move pinned labels out of stitching lines to another part of the block if need be. Always check to see if seams meet evenly for a neat triangle join, and carefully seam-rip, repin, and resew if need be. Now join 3A + 4A + 5A, then 2A + 3A. Press. You have completed the first fourth of your quilt top!

19. Join all rows in the 1B–5B, 6A–10A, and 6B–10B quadrants the same way. The quilt top is now ready to be put together.

20. Carefully pin quadrant 1A to quadrant 1B to create the upper half of your quilt top, matching seamlines. Stitch them together, supporting the weight of the quilt top so it doesn't pull your stitching line out of alignment. Press the seam to the left.

21. Repeat to carefully pin and stitch quadrant 6A and quadrant 6B together to form the lower half of your quilt top. Press the seam to the right.

22. Now, press both halves of your quilt top. Pin the halves together at each angle, seam, and block join, and carefully stitch them together. Check to make sure the long seam is secure, then press. Your quilt top is complete!

FINISH THE QUILT

23. Mark your quilt top for quilting using chalk, a fabric pen tested on scraps, or painter's tape. Layer the quilt top, batting, and backing, and quilt as desired. Note: For a full-size quilt this heavy meant for everyday use, I don't recommend hand- or machine-tying, or solely hand-quilting unless it's very densely stitched, as they're not as durable as sturdy machine-quilting.

24. If you are working with a longarm quilter, bring your unmarked quilt top, batting, and backing to her studio and collaborate on a design.

25. When you have finished quilting, stitch the perimeter of your quilt, then trim away the excess batting and backing.

26. Prepare handmade binding from fabric, or use premade ½-in. double-fold binding to machine-bind the quilt.

27. Add a special label celebrating the child who's receiving your quilt. Find lots of ideas at sewplusquilt.com.

make it simpler

Use just two fabrics, one that's bright and one that's light, to make this design. I've designed a mini version that highlights just the beautiful center star, using this simplified method, as a baby quilt celebrating a new addition to the family— Pearl and Everett's cousin Camille.

little star mini-quilt

WHAT YOU'LL NEED

- ½ yd. of a bright print; I used Rashida Coleman-Hale's butter-flies from her Moonlight collection
- ½ yd. of a light print; I used Mo Bedell's tiny diamonds from her Full Moon Lagoon collection
- Batting measuring 34 in. x 34 in.
- Backing measuring 34 in. x 34 in.; I used Lizzy House's pink Pearl Bracelets
- ¼ yd. of fabric for binding; I used Michael Miller's Aqua Cotton Couture

1. Cut one 15½-in. square and four 8½-in. squares from your bright fabric. Cut four 8-in. squares and four 8½-in. squares from your light fabric. Press.

2. Use the eight 8½-in. squares to make 8 bright/light HST blocks using the 2-at-a-time method. Press and trim these HSTs to 8 in. square.

3. Lay out the star, with the large bright fabric square in the center and 8 bright/light HST blocks radiating out to form the sawtooth star points. Then place one 8-in. light square at each of the 4 corners.

4. Assemble the top row (1) and bottom row (4), working from left to right. Press the row 1 seams to the left and row 4 seams to the right.

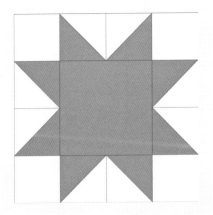

5. Now join the two star-point HST blocks at the right and left sides of the center square into vertical pairs.

6. Sew the left star-point pair to the left edge of the large center square and the right star-point pair to the right edge of the square. Press seams toward the center.

7. Pin and stitch row 1 to the top of the center section, matching all seams and angles, then pin and stitch row 4 to the bottom edge the same way. Press all seams toward the center.

8. Quilt your mini as desired. Nancy Stovall used the same beautiful pearl bracelet-inspired pattern on Little Star as she did for Pearl's Bright Star Quilt.

may your joys
outnumber your sorrows
wedding quilt

Finished block size: 10 in.
Finished size: 80 in. x 80 in.
Longarm quilted by Nancy Stovall with an orange peel design
Seam allowance: ¼ in.

THE LOG CABIN BLOCK REPRESENTS THE HOME, WITH A RED or yellow center square as the hearth fire or lamp that warms everyone inside and the "logs" of the cabin radiating outward to signify the sun shining on one side of the home and shadows cast on the other. I wanted to make a fresh quilt that drew on that rich tradition, but with a bright and celebratory palette rather than the dark and light pairings that create the distinctive visual pattern.

This quilt was a joy to sew, but it also became the backdrop to my husband, Andrew's, sudden and serious illness. Many days I had time just to piece a block or two, snip selvage ends, and make quick notes in my sketchbook in between caring for him and doing all the things to keep a family going. As I sewed, it reminded me of our vows to ease each other's sorrows as well as share in joys, and that dark and uncertain days inevitably lift to make room for sunlight again.

Andrew was the first one to see the finished quilt top; he said it was his favorite in the whole collection. I brought the top to Nancy for the beautiful quilting that would complete my labor of love—no longer just a theoretical idea of a pretty, colorful quilt to give dear friends or family, but marking the deeper meaning of this particular chapter in our 20 years together.

WHAT YOU'LL NEED

- Sewing + Quilting Kit (pp. 10–13)
- 32 fat quarters (FQs) of assorted solids or 8 yd. total of solids of your choice, if you want to use fewer colors; I used 32 Denyse Schmidt Modern Solids from Free Spirit
- ¼ yd. of contrast solid for center squares—traditionally red or yellow; I used Denyse Schmidt Modern Solids in Pineapple
- Two grocery-store size paper or reusable bags, or sturdy boxes
- 32 large safety pins
- Batting measuring 84 in. x 84 in.
- Backing measuring 84 in. x 84 in.
- ½ yd. of fabric for binding, or 342 in./9½ yd. of ½-in. double-fold binding tape

techniques used

Pressing, *pp. 24–25*

Cutting, *pp. 25–26*

Log cabin chain piecing, *p. 37*

Row assembly, *p. 50*

Binding, *pp. 47–49*

If you're quilting this project at home, you'll also baste, mark, and quilt, *pp. 53–55*

cutting key	A (assorted solids)	B (contrast solid)	C (solid fabric of your choice)
Logs	32 sets of eight or nine 2-in. x 22-in. strips		
Center squares		Four 2-in. x WOF strips	
Backing			84 in. x 84 in.
Binding			342 in. total of 2-in.-wide strips

CUTTING + PIECING

1. Press all the FQs, then cut them into eight or nine 2-in. strips, according to the Cutting Key on p. 133. Depending on the width of the FQ, some will easily yield 9 strips, while others are a bit too narrow and you'll have only 8. As you cut each color, safety-pin the folded strips together at one end so they stay together during the design process.

2. Cut the strips from the center square fabric, according to the Cutting Key.

3. Label your bags or boxes with a large, noticeable A and B, so you can sort colors as you use them.

4. Once all fabrics are cut and ready to piece, spread out the safety-pinned colors on your worktable or another convenient flat surface. Choose one color to start with (we will call this color A) and find another color that provides a good contrast—it doesn't have to be dramatically darker or lighter, but it should offer a vibrant or distinct tone that will create an interesting reflective block (color B). Once you have chosen your first two fabrics, A and B, unpin them and cut a 4-in. length of your center square color. (If you prefer, cut two 2-in. center squares rather than using a 4-in. strip.)

5. Begin a two-block chain-piece, stitching the 4-in. center square strip to color A with a ¼-in. seam allowance, right sides facing (though this may not matter with typical solids). Trim away the remaining strip of color A, and then use a rotary cutter and quilt ruler to cut the paired fabrics into 2 identical center squares joined to log 1. Finger-press the seams away from the center.

HERE'S MY ADVICE

This is optional, but I snipped off a narrow selvage end of each color as I used it and set it aside in a dish near my sewing machine. This was an easy way to see which colors I had used so far and what the overall color mix was looking like.

6. Chain-piece to add log 2 of color A to both blocks the same way, always adding new logs clockwise and pressing seams away from the center.

7. Switching to color B, chain-piece to add log 3 to both blocks, then add log 4, also in B. You'll have two identical one-tier log cabin blocks, each with A as the recessive color and B as the dominant color.

8. Press the blocks on the back and front, and then square up the blocks so their edges are straight and neat.

9. Chain-piece to add a second tier of color A (logs 5 and 6), then color B (logs 7 and 8), always working clockwise, adding the new strip to the side with the shortest log, and joining A to A and B to B.

10. You will now have two identical two-tier log cabin blocks. Press them on the back and front and square them up, then stack them together.

HERE'S MY ADVICE

If you cut small selvage swatches of your colors earlier, you can stitch them to a long strip of your center square fabric if you like, for a little souvenir. I arranged mine in color order, spaced about ¼ in. apart, on a 20-in. strip of pineapple yellow.

11. Continue chain-piecing the same way to add a third tier of logs, with logs 9 and 10 in color A and logs 11 and 12 in color B. Press and square up, trimming to 10½ in. square. These are blocks 1 + 2.

12. Now repin your remaining scraps and strips of color A so all of them are secured together, then do the same with B. You'll reuse these colors in new pairings during the second half of the block-piecing process. Place the previously used pinned set of color A strips into the B bag so it can be used as a color B (dominant) next time, and the previously used B into the A bag.

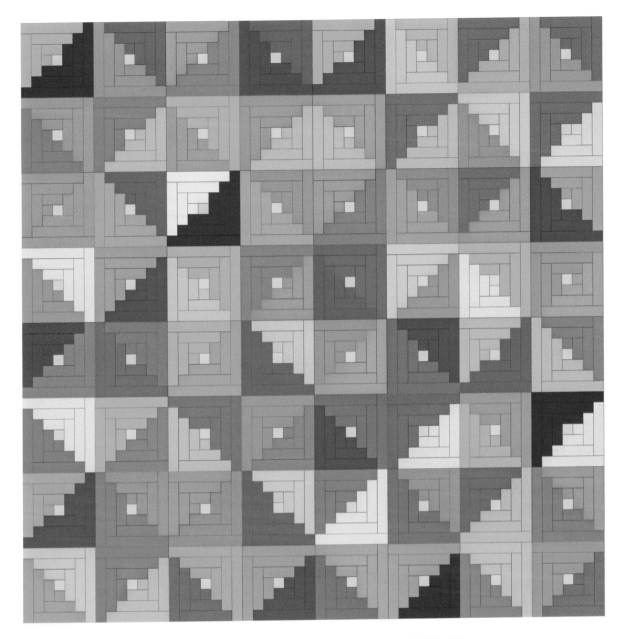

13. Choose two more colors from your worktable to use as a new A and B. Chain-piece two more identical blocks the same way, starting with a 4-in. strip of center square fabric stitched to color A, then cut into two paired center + log sections. Continue by following steps 6–10, pressing and trimming each new completed tier. Stack the completed blocks 3 + 4 with blocks 1 + 2, repin the color strips, and put them in the A or B bag they haven't been used for so you can draw them later.

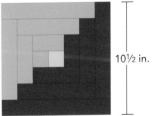

10½ in.

14. Continue pairing colors and chain-piecing blocks until you have used each color once, half as A and half as B, and have 32 blocks, each 10 in. square when completed. This is a great feeling—you're

choosing a color palette

Determining a color palette for a quilt is a very intuitive process and different for everyone. I chose my 32 colors from the beautiful Denyse Schmidt Modern Solids FQ collection, first eliminating the darkest darks and lightest lights. I wanted a rainbow effect, but with interesting shades like olive green, pale aqua, magenta, and coral included to balance the expected primary colors and make it feel more textured and engaging. I held FQ folds together and took photos of the palette, editing some out and adding in others, until I was happy with my color mix. I ended up leaning toward cool greens and blues as the most frequently used color families, with deep, warm reds, oranges, and yellows as a beautiful contrast, and browns as my occasional neutral.

If you're making this quilt as a gift, use the recipients' favorite colors as a starting point and add more compatible colors from there.

---

halfway done with piecing an amazing quilt! Pin a label to this stack that says first half, so you can use it for quick reference on which colors have already been used together and in which blocks, if you'd like to ensure variety.

15. Now you get to remix all 32 gorgeous colors in new pairings and in the opposite placement on the second round of blocks. Draw a color A randomly (remember, one that's already been used as a B previously), and then hold it next to several in your B bag until you find an interesting contrast. Don't reuse the same color pairings (unless you want to intentionally), but pair similar colors that you like the relationship between more than once. Some I found myself using several times—in various combinations of darker and lighter or more subdued and brighter—were orange/coral with blue/aqua, greens with purples, and red/oranges with pale, cool colors (sky blue, light green). There are no rules for this. Unlike a traditional log cabin block that might always use lighter fabrics as color A and darker as color B, mixing colors throughout defines the graphic pattern with more vibrancy and less expectedness.

16. Following steps 6–10, chain-piece blocks 33 + 34 (the first two in your remixed second half of your quilt), using your new colors A and B. Press and trim each completed tier, squaring up the blocks at 10½ in. square. Start a new stack of blocks beside the first half (not mixing in with them if possible). Save any leftover strips, safety-pinned together, off to the side of your worktable—there is no need to separate them by A and B after you've used each one twice.

17. Continue using one draw from bag A and one from B in new pairings to chain-piece blocks for the second half of the quilt. If you get mixed up with which colors you have already paired, check your first stack of blocks for reference.

make it simpler

Use just 16, or even 8, fabrics to make this quilt much more straightforward. You'd need 16 half-yd. or 8 yd. of solids for this simplified version. Vary your color pairings or make 4 of the same block each time, then group those together into a diamond.

18. When you get down to the last five or six of each of your A and B fabrics, make intentional pairings, so you don't inadvertently end up with a final block or two that are duplicates or contain two colors that are very similar.

19. Continue chain-piecing until you have 64 pressed, trimmed log cabin blocks that measure 10½-in. square.

ASSEMBLE THE QUILT TOP

20. Now it's time to design your layout! This was a challenging but very fun process for me. I set out the blocks quickly, in an allover repeating diamonds pattern using an 8 x 8 grid, and then began editing and changing block placement throughout the entire quilt. Take photos frequently to see if an area is pooling with bright, dark, light, or too much of the same color, or if identical blocks are too close. I probably took 20 photos throughout my process. Be sure to filter them to black and white from time to time to get a better sense of how the dark and light values read. Share photos with friends to get their feedback, too—I texted several layout photos to my PMQG friends Tamara, Petra, Heather, Nancy, and Michelle to get their thoughts, which was super helpful and encouraging.

21. When you are happy with your design, take a final photo, then label the rows 1–8, pinning numbered slips of paper to the leftmost block in each row, and then take a photo of that—it's very important to have for reference.

22. Stack the rows of blocks, with the numbered block on top, and organize them into piles labeled 1–8.

137

23. Begin assembling the rows, working from left to right, matching colors at the seamlines and stitching the blocks with a ¼-in. seam allowance. Set each row aside as you finish.

24. Press all rows with seams to one side—odd rows (1, 3, 5, 7) to the left and even (2, 4, 6, 8) to the right.

25. Pin rows 1 + 2 together, carefully matching all seams and color meetings, and nesting seams together. Stitch with a ¼-in. seam allowance. Check the back to make sure every block is sewn securely, without any wavy seams that veer too close to the raw edge of the fabrics. Note: In every other row seam, larger "diamonds" will meet within a block;

these seams will need to be pinned more carefully. The other rows' seams will simply need to be matched at seam lines.

26. Continue pinning and joining rows 3 + 4, 5 +6, and 7 + 8 the same way. (Full disclosure: I realized my row 3 was coming up short, and then I saw the missing block on the floor, where it had tumbled off my stack. I was so thankful for my clear reference photo that showed it should have been block 6 in the row! I seam-ripped two blocks to stitch in the missing block at the right spot.)

27. Carefully pin rows 1 + 2 to 3 + 4 and join them to create the upper half of the quilt top. Do the same to join rows 5 + 6 and 7 + 8.

take it further

Use your scraps to make a beautiful 16-in. log cabin pillow, this time setting the center "diamond" with the recessive log colors, surrounded by the dominant ones.

You'll need 44 in. total of 2-in.-wide strips for center squares and border fabric (I used Denyse Schmidt Modern Solids Pineapple, like the centers in my larger quilt), and two sets of leftover 2-in.-wide strips, each in eight assorted colors, for your logs. I used eight strips, about 14 in. total length each, in cool colors for my A logs (the smaller/recessive center diamond) and eight strips, about 16 in. total length each, in warm colors for my B logs (the background). I contrasted cool and warm tones. I especially liked them for texture and interest, but you could use darks and lights, two different color families, two colors only, or whatever appeals to you. This 14-in. or 16-in. length can be in one continuous strip or in varying lengths that add up to the total needed.

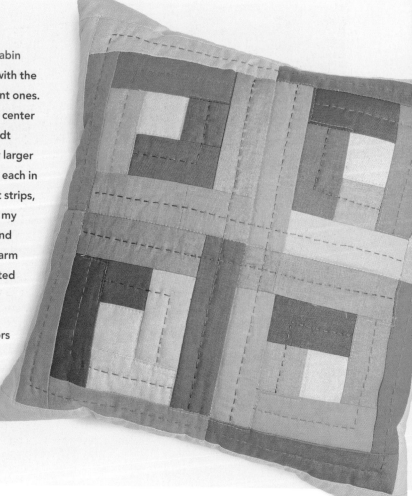

28. Pinning and sewing carefully, and supporting the weight of the quilt, join the two halves of the top together, using a ¼-in. seam allowance.

29. Press all seams away from the center (upward or downward), with rows 4 + 5 seam pressed downward. Press the front as well. You have finished your colorful quilt top!

FINISH THE QUILT

30. I collaborated with longarm quilter Nancy Stovall to find the simple, beautiful orange peel design that looks like a perfect dogwood flower repeated all over the quilt. It also uses concentric circles that reminded me of interlocked wedding rings. If you are quilting this quilt yourself, decide on your quilting pattern and mark it with chalk, a fabric marker, or washi or painter's tape.

31. Baste the quilt top, batting, and backing together. Quilt as desired, following your marked lines or tape.

32. Stitch the perimeter of the quilt, trim away the excess batting and backing, and machine-bind (see pp. 47–49).

33. Add a special label on the back to share your quilt's story or to celebrate the recipients. Find ideas at sewplusquilt.com.

center diamond wedding pillow

1. Cut four 2-in. squares from a strip of the center squares/border color, then use the first two to piece two different blocks, one at a time, with 2 tiers of logs, using your eight A and eight B colors once each and randomizing the placements; the blocks will be 7½ in. square when trimmed; use all 16 assorted colors once.

2. Now use your third and fourth center square to piece two more log cabin blocks, again using the whole collection of eight A and eight B colors only once, so there's lots of variety in your blocks.

3. Arrange the 4 blocks in a diamond layout, with the A colors meeting in the center to form a smaller diamond. Join blocks 1 + 2 and then 3 + 4, matching seams and colors, before joining the top and bottom rows. Press.

4. Add a 2-in. strip of border fabric to the left and right of the blocks, then add a 2-in. strip to the top and bottom. Press all seams away from the center.

5. Hand-baste to a 19-in. square of batting and 19-in. piece of muslin backing. Quilt or tie as desired. I machine-quilted an outline design around my center diamond, then another outline just to the outside of my border seams. Then I hand-quilted all my cool color logs in aqua perle cotton and did the same with my warm dominant background in coral perle cotton, following the lines of the logs. Carefully press, stitch the perimeter with a ¼-in. seam from the edge, and trim the extra backing

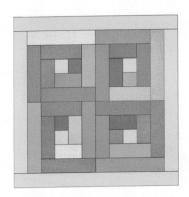

and batting. My pillow cover measured 18½ in. square.

6. Cut a square of backing fabric the same size as the cover (I used more Pineapple), add a 16-in. invisible zipper using the instructions on p. 30, and then use a ½-in. seam allowance to join the pillow front and back. I used a very lofty 16-in. down pillow that filled up my oversized cover, but if you have a lightweight or flat 18-in. pillow, you can use that instead.

anniversary mini-quilt

Finished block size: 3½ in. square (4 HSTs)
Finished size: 17 in. x 13 in.
Machine-quilted in an outline pattern
Seam allowance: ¼ in.

I'VE BEEN COLLECTING CALENDAR TEA TOWELS FOR YEARS. I love the designs and details, and they are useful as well as fun. I have vintage Vera calendars from the years my husband and I were born, and I bought new ones from my artist friends Rebecca Pearcy and Jessee Maloney for each of my kids, sewing a little button on each of our four birthdays. Our 12th wedding anniversary was last summer, and I wanted to make a fun mini-quilt that drew on the same idea as those beautiful textile calendars. I used some of my favorite quilting cotton prints in our wedding colors, pink and brown. You only need a 3½-in. square of each fabric, so the tiniest scraps go a long way!

I embroidered our wedding date (August 7, 2005) where the month would be if this were a calendar tea towel, but you can embellish this mini-quilt any way you like. You can also include more or fewer blocks—I liked the calendar-like symmetry of 12, but this would look great with 4, 9, 16, or any other number that creates a pleasing rectangle or square layout. Instead of wedding colors, choose any meaningful prints and patterns, scrap fabrics, or other special bits and pieces that tell your story.

WHAT YOU'LL NEED

- Sewing + Quilting Kit (pp. 10–13)
- Embroidery Kit (pp. 8–10); optional
- Twenty-four 3½-in. squares of quilting cotton; I used 12 different pink prints and two each of 6 brown prints
- 1 fat quarter (FQ) of background fabric; I used a pale pink from a cotton pillowcase
- Batting measuring 18 in. x 14 in.
- Backing measuring 18 in. x 14 in.; I used the same pink gingham as one of my blocks
- ⅛ yd. of fabric for binding, or 72 in./2 yd. of ½-in. double-fold binding tape; I used the same brown as one of my blocks

techniques used

Pressing, *pp. 24–25*

Cutting, *pp. 25–26*

4-at-a-time HST
method, *p. 44*

Sashing, *p. 45*

Borders, *pp. 45–46*

Embroidery, *pp. 18–23*

Basting, *p. 46*

Machine-quilting, *p. 54*

Binding, *pp. 47–49*

cutting key	A (brown prints)	B (pink prints)	C (solid pink)
HST blocks	Twelve 3½-in. squares, two each of six prints	Twelve 3½-in. squares, each a different print	
Sashing			Two 1-in. x WOF strips
Borders			Two 1½-in. WOF strips
Backing		18-in. x 14-in. piece of one print	
Binding	72 in. total of 2-in.-wide strips		

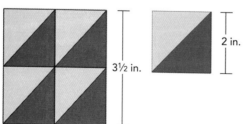

3½ in.

 2 in.

HERE'S MY ADVICE

Avoid using strong directional or text prints in this project, as the 4-at-a-time HST method will spin them around quite a bit. The scrappy nature of the project keeps it lighthearted and fun, and any intentional embellishments like embroidering names or dates stand out beautifully on a simpler fabric background in the mix, like gold floss on my crosshatch brown that almost reads as a solid.

CUTTING + PIECING

1. Cut and press the fabrics according to the Cutting Key.

2. Pair the 3½-in. squares in sets of two. I used all different pink prints, from vintage gingham to modern quilting cottons, and repeated each of my brown prints once.

3. Use the 4-at-a-time method to make 4 small HST blocks from each set. Press, cut, and trim each one into a 2-in. block.

4. Now, arrange the first set of 4 mini-blocks into the HST layout of your choice. I set mine as triangles, all oriented in the same direction (a simple block layout traditionally called Everlasting Tree or Geese in Flight), but you may like to arrange yours as a diamond, pinwheel, or any other 4-HST setting.

5. Pin and stitch first the upper two and then the lower two blocks together. Pin to match seamlines and nest seams, then stitch the two rows at the center to form a 4-HST block.

6. Repeat to join the rest of your single HSTs into 11 more 4-HST blocks. Press on both back and front, and square up the blocks if any of the bias edges are wavy.

ASSEMBLE THE QUILT TOP

7. Now you'll decide on your layout. As with my Pinwheels Baby Quilt (p. 108), I arranged these blocks so the repeating darker fabrics appeared once in the top half and once in the bottom half of the layout and weren't too close to each other. Move blocks around until you like the flow and balance, then take a photo for reference. For a quilt this tiny, you can pin numbered slips to the leftmost blocks in each row, or simply leave them in the layout until you reach for the next row to sew in order.

8. Stitch the three blocks in row 1 together, working from left to right and adding a strip of 1-in. sashing between the blocks. Trim the sashing flush with the block each time. Press the seams toward the sashing, and then press the front of the row.

9. Repeat to join rows 2, 3, and 4 the same way.

10. Now join the bottom edge of row 1 to a strip of sashing, trimming the strip flush with the last block when you finish. Stitch the top edge of row 2 to the other long side of the sashing, pinning to match all block edges and pressing seams toward the sashing each time.

11. Continue to join rows 3 and 4 the same way, then join all four rows together. Press.

12. Stitch a 1½-in. border to the top and then the bottom edges of the quilt top, trimming the ends flush with the blocks. Then stitch borders to the left and right sides the same way. Press all seams toward the borders.

FINISH THE QUILT

13. If you'd like to embroider anything special on your mini-quilt, you can do that now. I embroidered our wedding date on one of the blocks with metallic gold floss, using the backstitch and putting the patchwork in a hoop to keep the fabric smooth and stable. You can write or draw your design with a fabric marker (as with Memento Embroidery Artwork, p. 62) or embellish however you like.

14. Baste the mini-quilt top, batting, and backing together. I hand-basted mine since it was so small.

15. Quilt as desired. I machine-quilted a simple outline pattern all around each of the blocks, stitching from top to bottom and side to side within the sashing and turning all corners to follow the square shapes.

16. Stitch the perimeter of the quilt, trim away the excess batting and backing, and bind (pp. 47–49).

make it simpler

Use just two fabrics for your HSTs for a minimalist design and effortless layout—¼ yd. each will be more than enough, with scraps left over.

take it further

Make this quilt to celebrate a special anniversary—20th, 25th, 30th, 50th, or any other milestone—with that many blocks!

birthday mini-quilt

Finished block size: 3½ in. square
Finished size: 16 in. by 16 in.
Seam allowance: ¼ in.

THIS ADORABLE MINI-QUILT IS A JOY TO PIECE WITH JUST eight tiny string blocks to make. Four of those are remixed into half-square triangles (HSTs) for a fun change of pace. It draws on the same piecing techniques I used in both the Golden Rays Quilt (p. 120) and Bright Star Quilt (p. 126), but since it's so much smaller, it takes a fraction of the time to make!

Change the feel of this wall quilt to match your celebration, changing the bright mix to a more sophisticated color palette, going monochromatic, or using all solids.

WHAT YOU'LL NEED

- Sewing + Quilting Kit (pp. 10–13)
- Embroidery Kit (pp. 8–10); optional for hand-quilting
- ¼ yd. of muslin for foundation piecing
- Twelve 1-in. x WOF strips of assorted prints, repeated or all different
- ¼ yd. of background fabric; I used XOXO in On the Rocks by Rashida Coleman-Hale
- Batting measuring 18 in. x 18 in.
- Backing measuring 18 in. x 18 in.; I used the same as my background fabric
- ⅛ yd. of fabric for binding, or 2¼ yd. of prepared ½-in. double-fold binding

cutting key	A (muslin for foundation piecing)	B (assorted prints)	C (background print)
String blocks	Four EACH 4-in. squares and 4½-in. squares	Twelve 1-in. x WOF strips	
Background			Four EACH 4-in. squares and 4½-in. squares
Borders			Two 1½-in. WOF strips
Backing			18 in. x 18 in. square
Binding		Two 2-in. x WOF strips of one print	

techniques used

Pressing, *pp. 24–25*

Cutting, *pp. 25–26*

Trimming, *p. 35*

String piecing, *pp. 40–41*

2-at-a-time HST
method, *pp. 42–43*

Quilt assembly, *pp. 50–53*

Binding, *pp. 47–49*

Borders, *pp. 45–46*

Basting, *p. 53*

Machine-quilting, *p. 54*

Hand-quilting, *p. 55*

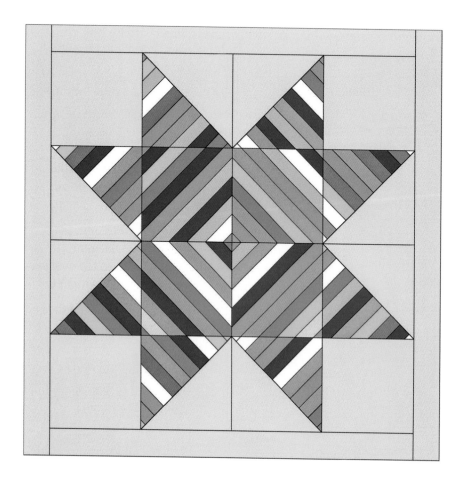

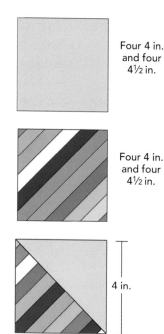

Four 4 in.
and four
4½ in.

Four 4 in.
and four
4½ in.

4 in.

CUTTING + PIECING

1. Cut and press all fabrics you'll use to construct the blocks and background for your mini-quilt (see the Cutting Key, p. 144).

2. Piece the first four string blocks on 4-in. squares of muslin, using the 1-in. strips of fabric and alternating prints for a variety of colors and movement. I arranged mine so they didn't appear more than once within the same block. You will need to use about nine strips of fabric to piece each of the four 4-in. blocks, and your finished diagonal stripes will measure ½ in. wide within the blocks.

3. Now piece four slightly larger string blocks on 4½-in. squares of foundation muslin, using about 11 strips to make the 4½-in. blocks. All eight blocks will appear the same way, but the first four will be ½ in. smaller than the second set.

4. Press, trim, and square up all string blocks. Set the 4-in. blocks aside.

5. Pair each of the 4½-in. string blocks and 4½-in. background squares to make a total of 8 HST blocks using the 2-at-a-time method (pp. 42–43). You'll use your pieced string blocks just like plain fabric squares. Orient them right sides facing, so your diagonal seamline will be perpendicular to (not with) the piecing stripes' direction for a pretty effect (see the diagram above). Mark the diagonal, sew ¼ in. on either side of the line, and then cut on the line. Press seams toward the background fabric; trim each HST to 4 in. square.

6. You should now have 8 HST blocks, 4 string blocks, and 4 background squares, each measuring 4 in. square. Press each block.

ASSEMBLE THE QUILT TOP

7. Arrange the star layout. Start by positioning the 4 string blocks so the diagonals form a diamond in the center of the star. Then place the 8 HSTs around the center square, two at each side, so they form sawtooth star points. Arrange each section so the diagonals run in the same direction for a pleasing effect. If any of the same fabrics are touching, rearrange your blocks until you have a nice variety. Finally, place the four plain background squares at the corners to finish the quilt top design. Take a photo for reference.

8. Label the rows 1–4, and pin a numbered label onto the leftmost block in each row. Stack them and assemble the rows one by one. Press the seams on the odd rows (1 and 3) to the left and on even rows (2 and 4) to the right.

9. Join rows 1 + 2, then 3 + 4. Press. Sew the rows together to form the star.

10. Sew a border to the top of the star, trim the extra, and use it as a border for the bottom edge of the star. Press seams toward the borders.

11. Add borders to the left and right of the star in the same way. Press the mini-quilt top.

FINISH THE QUILT

12. Mark any quilting lines. I chose to outline the star with machine-quilting in a matching thread color, so I didn't need to mark my top.

13. Layer the top, batting, and backing, and baste. Quilt as desired. After I finished my machine-quilting, I hand-quilted with running stitches in gold perle cotton just outside of the machine-stitching.

14. Stitch the perimeter of the mini-quilt and then square it up, trimming away excess batting and backing.

15. Prepare handmade binding from two 2-in. x WOF strips of fabric, or use 2¼ yd. of premade ½-in. double-fold bias binding to bind your quilt.

make it simpler

Simply cut a focus fabric and a background fabric into four 4-in. and four 4½-in. blocks instead of piecing string blocks. Make eight 4-in. HST blocks the same way, using contrast 4½-in. squares of focus fabric (instead of pieced string blocks) and background fabric, and assemble your star.

take it further

For a beautiful effect, add more hand-quilting in a variety of colors, radiating out from the original star lines.

147

courthouse steps housewarming quilt

Finished block size: 60 in. x 64 in.
Finished size: 59 in. x 63 in.
Topstitched and perimeter-stitched
Seam allowance: ½ in.

WHAT COULD BE COZIER FOR A NEW HOME THAN A WARM wool quilt for your bed? This beautiful design is a single Courthouse Steps block, expanded to a generous scale so the striking geometric lines are bold and eye-catching.

I originally pieced this design improvisationally, starting with the center square and working outward to add symmetrical "steps" in gray and aqua jacquard wool fabrics (see "Take It Further" on p. 152). I didn't measure anything the whole time, and I finished the quilt in a single Saturday! When my friend Robin moved into her new house, she asked if I'd re-create my original Courthouse Steps for her, and we chose a new palette of desert colors—sage green, deep rust red, and vibrant orange, like her property in Central Oregon. It was fun to remake this intentionally, patterning it out with consistent measurements so it was easier to follow.

WHAT YOU'LL NEED

- Sewing + Quilting Kit (pp. 10–13)
- One 6-in. x 6-in. piece of a wool focus fabric (A) for the center square; this can match the main color fabrics or be a contrast
- 1½ yd. or more of 60-in.-wide medium-weight wool fabrics in a main color family (B) for the central hourglass design; you can include assorted solids or jacquard patterns, either blanket header strips at least 6 in. across or all one blanket section. I chose four different wool fabrics for my steps and used between one and four 6-in. x WOF strips of each. See the cutting diagram for how I cut and pieced my version
- 1¼ yd. or more of 60-in.-wide medium-weight wool fabrics in a background color (C); I used all the same fabric—a sage green solid wool
- Backing measuring approximately 63 in. x 67 in.; I used a lightweight worsted wool

techniques used

Cutting, *pp. 25–26*

Courthouse steps
piecing, *p. 36*

Clipping corners, *p. 29*

Topstitching, *p. 27*

Edgestitching, *p. 27*

cutting key	A (wool focus fabric; can be the same as one of the B fabrics or different)	B (assorted wool fabrics in a vibrant color palette)	C (wool fabrics in one or more muted background colors)	Lightweight wool
Courthouse steps	6-in. x 6-in. center square	Nine 6-in. x 60-in. strips	Nine 5-in. x 60-in. strips	
Backing				65 in. x 68 in. (can be pieced)

working with wool

Wool presses beautifully with steam or when sprayed with distilled water, and it sews like butter. Do keep your fabric weights consistent within a quilt top or project, so lightweight areas don't become "soft spots."

If you are using apparel-weight or lightweight jacquard fabrics, cut the strips the correct width and then press, align, and pin them to a medium or blanket-weight fabric backing and stitch the perimeter to join them as one fabric.

CUTTING

1. Press and cut your wool fabrics into strips the width of the fabric (WOF). You'll need a 6-in. x 6-in. center square of fabric A, nine 6-in. x WOF strips of the main color fabric B, and nine 5-in. x WOF strips of fabric C—the contrast steps to the right and left of the quilt.

ASSEMBLE THE QUILT TOP

2. Begin with the center square of fabric A. Add the first two "steps" by sewing a strip of fabric C to first the left and then the right of the square, with right sides facing, either precutting or using the snip and flip approach (sewing the strip, then trimming the excess fabric flush with the edge of your quilt top). Wool fabric is relatively thick, so sew with a slightly longer than normal straight stitch and a ½-in. seam allowance, pressing seams away from the center square and then topstitching them down to catch all layers before continuing to piece the next "steps." Square up the first three joined fabrics.

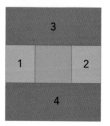

3. Hold or pin a strip of fabric B to the top of the block to form the third "step," with right sides facing; sew, then trim the strip flush with the edge of the block, and clip seam allowances at the corner to reduce bulk. Repeat with a strip of B at the bottom of the block to form the fourth "step." Press seams away from the center and topstitch through all layers— you may want to increase your stitch length for sewing through all four layers, which on my machine is a 4.0 or 4.5. Square up.

4. Continue adding strips of fabric to the top and bottom as before, and add C strips only to the sides (see the diagram, facing page). It's best if you trim away the bulk of the last seams before adding the next strip (see "Here's My Advice" below).

HERE'S MY ADVICE

To avoid bulk, clip the ends of the doubled seam allowances in your wool patchwork. Due to the weight of wool, it's more difficult to topstitch over and then piece new "steps" to thick layered seams; trimming at the back makes this easier.

5. Keep building your Courthouse Steps quilt until you are happy with the overall size. I added five rounds of "steps" to the top and bottom and six rounds of "steps" to the right and left. The joining seams and topstitching get longer the more strips you add, so press the back and pin at the front to make that process easier. The quilt will also get heavier, so be careful to fully support its weight on your sewing table or a chair as you sew.

6. When you have finished piecing the quilt top, square up the edges and corners and trim away bulk from the seams that intersect the outer edges of the quilt. Press.

make it simpler

Use just two wool fabrics, like big sections of recycled blankets, to make this design. Cut or tear one into 432 in./12 yd. total of 6-in.-wide strips—seven 6-in. strips from a 60-in.-wide blanket, for example. You'll use these for a center square and the vibrant top and bottom "steps." Cut or tear the other into 522 in./14½ yd. total of 5-in.-wide strips, or nine strips of a 60-in.-wide blanket (these will be the contrast left and right "steps"). Build the courthouse steps design the same way, piecing together shorter strips for length if needed as the steps grow in length.

HERE'S MY ADVICE

To achieve the size of the "steps" as the pattern grows, you will need to join pieces for the longest sections, measuring approximately 66 in. long and pieced from a 60-in. width plus a 7-in. section. Stitch them right sides facing with a ½-in. seam allowance, press or fold the seams to one side, and topstitch to finish.

FINISH THE QUILT

7. Now prepare your quilt back. If needed, join several sections together to achieve a big enough piece, sewing with a ½-in. seam allowance, right sides facing. Press seams to one side, and topstitch just as you did on the quilt top.

8. Lay the quilt back on a large flat surface, right side up. Now lay the quilt top over it, right side down, and align the two layers together so they're neat and the edges generally match. Pin all around the perimeter, leaving an 8-in. opening at the bottom. Carefully turn the pinned quilt and backing over to check the back. If it's pulling, creased, or off grain, gently unpin that section and realign.

9. Using a longer straight stitch, 3.5 on my machine, sew around the perimeter of the quilt ½ in. from the edge; sew smoothly over the seams. Stop at the opening, leaving it unsewn. Check the back to make sure there are no tucks or uneven areas; gently seam-rip and re-sew any sections if needed.

10. Trim any excess backing and clip the corners.

11. Turn the quilt right side out through the opening, shaking it gently so it settles smoothly into the joined layers. Ease the corners open with a pencil or chopstick so they are neat and square. Press all around the outer edges of the quilt, and pin the perimeter together neatly for a smooth, neatly finished quilt. Fold ½ in. of both layers to the inside of the quilt at the opening, and pin securely.

12. Using a longer stitch length, stitch the perimeter of the quilt again as a victory lap, sealing the opening and backstitching at the beginning and end to hold the seam securely.

13. Press or shake out and your quilt is finished.

take it further

Make a matching pillow with your leftover wool scraps. I pieced mine in gray and aqua strips from my first improvisational quilt.

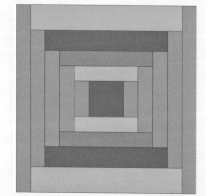

You'll need a 4-in. x 4-in. center square and assorted strips of wool in one color palette for the top and bottom "steps." I used about 30 in. total of 2½-in.-wide strips (matching logs 3 + 4, and 7 + 8) and about 60 in. total of 3-in. strips (logs 11+ 12 and 15 + 16). For the left and right "steps," I used about 112 in. total of

2½-in. strips, all in one contrast color (light gray).

Construct your mini version of the Courthouse Steps block the same way as the quilt size, joining steps to build the block outward and topstitching all seams. I made mine 18½ in. square. You don't need to quilt or use batting for this block, since the topstitching will make the patchwork strong and cohesive.

Finish with an invisible zipper (p. 30) and 18½-in. backing for an 18-in. pillow.

resources

Here are some of my favorite shops, books, websites, and other resources for embroidery, sewing, and quilting!

CONTRIBUTORS

Denyse Schmidt Quilts
dsquilts.com

Rebecca Ringquist of Dropcloth
dropclothsamplers.com

Nancy Stovall of Just Quilting
justquiltingpdx.com

Jenn Sturiale of Stitcharama
stitcharama.com

Kelly Cole of Vintage Fabric Studio
vintagefabricstudio.com

Michelle Freedman
instagram.com/stitchwellandprosper

SHOPS

Bolt
boltfabricboutique.com

Cozyblue Handmade
cozybluehandmade.com

Fabric Depot
fabricdepot.com

Fancy Tiger Crafts
fancytigercrafts.com

Joann Fabrics
joann.com

Pendleton Woolen Mill Store
thewoolenmillstore.blogspot.com

Purl Soho
purlsoho.com

Snuggly Monkey
snugglymonkey.com

BOOKS

EMBROIDERY, EMBELLISHMENT & EXTRAS

Button It Up by Susan Beal

Embroidered Effects and *Sublime Stitching* by Jenny Hart

Embroidery Companion by Alicia Paulson

Hand Dyed by Anna Joyce

The Little Book of Basic Embroidery by Alison Glass

Rebecca Ringquist's Embroidery Workshops by Rebecca Ringquist

Stamp Stencil Paint by Anna Joyce

SEWING

1, 2, 3 Sew by Ellen Luckett Baker

Alison Glass Appliqué by Alison Glass

Handmade Style by Anna Graham

Hand-Stitched Home and *Sewing for all Seasons* by Susan Beal

Martha Stewart's Encyclopedia of Sewing and Fabric Crafts by Martha Stewart

Print Pattern Sew by Jen Hewett

School of Sewing by Shea Henderson

Sewing Machine Secrets and *Sewing Solutions* by Nicole Vasbinder

How to Speak Fluent Sewing by Christine Haynes

You and Your Sewing Machine by Bernie Tobisch

QUILTING

1, 2, 3 Quilt by Ellen Luckett Baker

Denyse Schmidt Quilts and *Modern Quilts, Traditional Inspiration* by Denyse Schmidt

First Steps to Free-Motion Quilting by Christina Cameli

Lucky Spool's Essential Guide to Modern Quilt Making edited by Susanne Woods

Modern Log Cabin Quilting by Susan Beal

The Modern Quilt Workshop by Weeks Ringle and Bill Kerr

Patchwork Essentials: The Half-Square Triangle by Jeni Baker

The Practical Guide to Patchwork and *Modern Patchwork* by Elizabeth Hartman

Quilting Modern by Jacquie Gering and Katie Pedersen

Walk by Jacquie Gering

Wise Craft Quilts by Blair Stocker

RESOURCES

sew + quilt
sewplusquilt.com and
#sewplusquilt on Instagram
Printable quilt design pages to color, new versions of my favorite projects, lots of ideas for framing your embroidery and displaying your quilts, and everything else I couldn't fit into this book. I'd love to see your projects! Tag them #sewplusquilt.

Creativebug
creativebug.com
Hundreds of amazing craft, sewing, and quilting classes, including my beginner-friendly log cabin quilting series, and several projects from sew + quilt.

Portland Modern Quilt Guild
portlandmodernquiltguild.com
My local guild offers inspiration, friendship, creativity, an amazing block-of-the-month series, and wonderful presentations and workshops. Visit us or find your nearest MQG chapter at themodernquiltguild.com.

Quilt Canvas
quiltcanvas.com
I designed all the quilts in my book with this easy-to-use online subscription site; change scale or color, rotate blocks, and try out fabric swatches in a rainbow of colors.

Threads magazine
Threadsmagazine.com
The premier sewing magazine from Taunton Press, with helpful tips, video tutorials, projects, reviews, and so much more.

index